A LITERARY FRONTIERS
NO. 34

ART AND THE ACCIDENTAL IN ANNE TYLER

JOSEPH C. VOELKER

ART AND THE ACCIDENTAL
IN ANNE TYLER

UNIVERSITY OF MISSOURI PRESS

COLUMBIA AND LONDON

Copyright © 1989 by
The Curators of the University of Missouri
University of Missouri Press, Columbia, Missouri 65211
Printed and bound in the United States of America

Library of Congress Cataloging-in-Publication Data

Voelker, Joseph C.
     Art and the accidental in Anne Tyler / Joseph C. Voelker.

          p.   cm.—(A Literary frontiers edition ; no. 34)
          ISBN 0–8262–0716–2 (alk. paper)
          1. Tyler, Anne—Criticism and interpretation.   I. Title.
II. Series.
PS3570.Y45Z94   1989   89–4849
813'.54—dc20   CIP

∞™ This paper meets the minimum requirements of
the American National Standard for Permanence of Paper
for Printed Library Materials, Z39.48, 1984.

Designer: Barbara J. King
Typesetter: Connell-Zeko Type & Graphics
Printer: Thomson-Shore, Inc.
Binder: Thomson-Shore, Inc.
Type face: Palatino

5   4   3   2   1   94   93   92   91   90   89

IN LOVING MEMORY OF
Barbara DeAnn Hess

CONTENTS

Acknowledgments   xi

I Introduction   1

II North Carolina Novels: *If Morning Ever Comes,
     The Tin Can Tree, A Slipping-Down Life*   15

III *The Clock Winder*   48

IV *Celestial Navigation*   67

V *Searching for Caleb*   89

VI *Earthly Possessions*   106

VII *Dinner at the Homesick Restaurant*   125

VIII *The Accidental Tourist*   147

IX *Breathing Lessons*   165

Bibliography   179

Index   183

ACKNOWLEDGMENTS

I would like to express my gratitude to those people who have been helpful in this undertaking. Heartfelt thanks are due to my wife, Cathleen, for finding me the requisite hours and for reading the manuscript; to Franklin and Marshall College, for generous financial and library support; to my research assistant, Matthew Struckmeyer, and to two of his fellow students, Heather Fitzgerald and Alexis Kays, who taught me about Anne Tyler; to our department secretary, Arleen Faust; and to a number of friends and colleagues, whose criticism and suggestions were invaluable: Sanford Pinsker, Michael Roth, Paula Bresler, and Howard Kaye.

Acknowledgment is extended to Alfred A. Knopf for permission to quote from the novels of Anne Tyler.

ART AND THE ACCIDENTAL IN ANNE TYLER

I INTRODUCTION

IN his widely read study of American leadership, *Puritan Boston and Quaker Philadelphia*, E. Digby Baltzell defined the dominant attributes of two opposed American sensibilities.[1] Bostonians, he found, established enduring institutions out of a conviction of human depravity, and they countered the natural American tendency toward egalitarianism with an aristocratic insistence on the need for a hierarchical ordering of power, a governing of the nonelect among whom diabolic voices whispered unceasingly. Puritan culture inspired an icy egotism in its elite, but it supplied a growing nation with citizens who found public and professional service to be evidence of their own divine election. Philadelphians, on the other hand, held firmly to a conviction of human perfectibility and allowed a social organism to evolve that reflected their sense of God's potential presence in every soul. Quakers valued tolerance and humility, and an antinomian, radically democratic streak in their culture came to preclude high achievement in the public realm, robbed them, as it were, of a necessary arrogance.

Differences between the two cultures took very specific forms, ones that have persisted into the twentieth century, despite the abandonment of theocratic structures. New England Puritans were paternalistic; Philadelphians (and their fellow Quakers in New Jersey and North Carolina) tended to practice gender equality. Puritans looked to formally endowed spiritual authorities and a transcendent God knowable through doctrine; Quakers trusted to conscience and the spontaneous and commonly available direction of an Inner Light. Puritans

---

1. E. Digby Baltzell, *Puritan Boston and Quaker Philadelphia* (New York: Free Press, 1979).

1

sought evidence of salvation in their worldly vocations; Quakers tended to withdraw from the world in a monasticism that embraced simplicity but eschewed neither wealth nor marriage. While Puritans were sexually intolerant, Baltzell observed, Quakers tended toward a "mild sexlessness," an absence of hysteria (or obsession) about the subject. Baltzell wrote: "*The Scarlet Letter,* I have always suspected, could not have been written in, or about, Philadelphia."[2] When Baltzell set out to project Quaker culture into a secular twentieth century, he observed, "An egalitarian religious ethic such as the Quakers postulated . . . will be far more likely to be associated with lack of authority, or extreme individualism, once the belief in the absolute authority of God has been lost."[3] With the ebbing of a sense of divine presence, Quakerism has evolved into a cultural style characterized by tolerance verging on quietism.

There is pleasure in imagining that these cultural tendencies have a kind of persistence in two of our most masterful fictional realists, John Updike and Anne Tyler. Born and raised a Lutheran in Shillington, Pennsylvania, Updike attended Harvard University. Then he stayed on in a New England that, haunted by Hawthorne, gave free rein to the Protestant aspect of his imagination and provided the steepled backdrop for his lyricism and his abiding obsessions, sex and the demonic, conjoined in that favorite Updikean metaphor, the witch. Tyler, born in Minnesota, grew up in an experimental Quaker community outside Raleigh, North Carolina, a circumstance she considers formative. In an autobiographical essay entitled "Still Just Writing," she says: "I know a poet who says that in order to be a writer, you have to have had rheumatic fever, but I believe that any kind of setting-apart situation will do as well. In my case, it was emerging from that commune—really an experimental Quaker

2. Ibid., 102.
3. Ibid., 95.

community in the wilderness—and trying to fit into the outside world."[4]

In both her fiction and her life, Tyler has reflected the distrust of glamour, the quiet resistance toward moral authority, the conviction of human goodness, and the calm insouciance toward sexuality that Baltzell identifies as essentially Quaker. An Updike novel naturally gravitates toward hellfire sermon. Updike parodies various fuzzy spiritualities (including even Marxist Muslim fundamentalism in *The Coup* and an addled adaptation of Hinduism in *S*). One senses behind them the presence of *Rabbit, Run*'s Reverend Kruppenbach, ready to clarify and denounce. The Tyler novel is a Friends meeting,[5] its speech issuing, as Tyler has repeatedly stated, from "some clear, swept space inside me."[6] Invariably, Tyler hands over spontaneous inspiration to one of her characters, none of whom is denied at least the potential to see and speak the gently surprising truth, each of whom is permitted captainship of his or her destiny within the confines of a random and ungovernable external world. Tyler has cannily observed the abdication of authority at the heart of her emotional connection to her characters— the practice of tolerance become an artistic method:

> What's hard is that there are times when your characters simply won't obey you. Nearly every writer I've heard of says that: not one has satisfactorily explained it. Where did those little paper people get so much power?
>
> I'll have in mind an event for them—a departure, a

4. See "Still Just Writing," in Janet Sternburg, ed., *The Writer on Her Work: Contemporary Women Writers Reflect on Their Art and Situation*, 11. Tyler described some of the circumstances of her childhood in the Quaker community in a letter to Stella Nesanovich. See Nesanovich's "The Individual in the Family: A Critical Introduction to the Novels of Anne Tyler," viii.

5. Tyler's description of her study as a "stern, white cubicle" points up its similarity to a Quaker meetinghouse. See "Because I Want More than One Life," G7.

6. Tyler, "Still Just Writing," 11.

wedding, a happy ending. I write steadily toward that event, but when I reach it, everything stops. I can't go on. Sentences come out stilted, dialogue doesn't sound real. Every new attempt ends up in the wastebasket. I try again from another angle, and then another, until I'm forced to admit it: The characters just won't allow this. I'll have to let the plot go their way. And when I do, everything falls into place.[7]

Central to the contemporary novelist's conception of writing is the idea of giving voice to the consciousness of a character. Updike and Tyler, despite the realist assumptions they share, their mimetic impulse, their common wish to practice an accessible art, differ radically in the nature of the consciousness to which they give voice. While both succeed wonderfully in rendering the surface of contemporary middle-class life, the persistence of America's two opposing theological visions defines their difference. The Updikean narrative voice is rooted—however remotely—in a culture founded upon the conviction of sin. Updike disinvites the tolerance so central to Tyler. What Rabbit thinks when Rabbit is alone is a stream carrying a mixed flotsam of grace and vileness. Rabbit is meant to outrage, and Updike's best efforts serve to prevent the reader's bland, sophisticated indulgence in the name of some godless therapeutic. Updike offers back to readers their own worst thoughts, daring them to acknowledge those thoughts as their own. Consider Rabbit in his Toyota—racist, horny, power-happy, incestuous, and metaphysical:

The vanished white giants as they filled Brewer into its grid named these higher streets that Eisenhower crosses for fruits and the seasons of the year: Winter, Spring, Summer, but no Fall Street. For three months twenty years ago Rabbit lived on Summer with a woman, Ruth Leonard. There he fathered the girl he saw today, if that was his daughter. There is no getting away; our sins, our seed, coil back. The disco music shifts to the Bee Gees, white men who have done this

7. "Because I Want More than One Life," G7.

wonderful thing of making their voices sound like black women. "Stayin' Alive" comes on with all that amplified throbbleo and a strange nasal whining underneath: the John Travolta theme song. Rabbit still thinks of him as one of the Sweathogs from Mr. Kotter's class but for a while back there last summer the U.S.A. was one hundred per cent his, every twat under fifteen wanting to be humped by a former sweat-hog in the back seat of a car parked in Brooklyn. He thinks of his own daughter getting into the back seat of the Corolla, bare leg up to her ass. He wonders if her pubic hair is ginger in color like her mother's was. That curve where a tender entire woman seems an inch away around a kind of corner, where no ugly penis hangs like sausage on the rack, blue-veined. Her eyes his blue: wonderful to think that he has been turned into cunt, a secret message carried by genes all that way through all these comings and goings all these years, the bloody tunnel of growing and living, of staying alive. He better stop thinking about it, it fills him too full of pointless excitement. Some music does that.[8]

Rabbit's thoughts respond to promptings from below. The passage contrasts pointedly with the relative serenity of Tyler's prose, the absence in her characters' consciousness of any real psychic undertow. Tyler is just as likely as Updike to sneak up on characters in an idle moment and eavesdrop inside their brains; both will exploit the opportunity to record the passing minutiae of the culture, its rock-and-roll titles and the brand names of shampoos. But Tyler's characters will remain disengaged, observant, usually moved to nothing stronger than whimsy or sadness. Updike's will be maddened by lyric, surprised by sin.

It makes sense, then, that Updike, in his review of *Dinner at the Homesick Restaurant*, congratulated the mimetic accuracy but worried at the absence of obsession in Tyler's previous work. He wrote in the *New Yorker*:

Anne Tyler, too, has sought brightness in the ordinary,

8. *Rabbit Is Rich* (New York: Fawcett Crest, 1981), 30.

and her art has needed only the darkening that would give her beautifully sketched shapes solidity. So evenly has her imagination moved across the details of the mundane that the novels, each admirable, sink in the mind without leaving an impression of essential, compulsive, subject matter, the agoraphobia portrayed in "Celestial Navigation" being something of an exception, and perhaps the southward tug felt in "Searching for Caleb" and "Earthly Possessions."[9]

This is a rich misunderstanding. In the interest of ecumenism, a Puritan goes to meeting, but he is puzzled at the apparent nonproceedings. There is good evidence that Tyler and Updike radically disagree on the fundamental question of consciousness. In fact, Updike occasionally makes use of Tyler's figuration of the self as a "clear swept space" inside, but always to antithetical ends. In the very last minutes of *Rabbit, Run,* for instance, Rabbit "feels his inside as very real suddenly, a pure blank space in the middle of a dense net. *I don't know,* he kept telling Ruth; he doesn't know, what to do, where to go, what will happen." His response, of course, is futile, directionless flight, for the one place Rabbit cannot delight in finding a hole is inside himself.

Compare that moment to a comment by Ansel Green, the wheedling hypochondriac of Tyler's *The Tin Can Tree.* He turns to his brother and says, "Sometimes I think your mind is just a clean, clean slate, James." James calmly responds, "I keep it that way."[10] A self-composed vacancy was the subject of Tyler's novels from the very first, but it was only with *Celestial Navigation,* and the rendering of the mind of the agoraphobe Jeremy Pauling, that her technique caught up with her fictional subject—a spiritual white noise, a happy idling of the biological entity into which the voice of inspiration has opportunity to intrude. Each of Jeremy's sections of the novel records a coming-into-focus, a short epoch of alertness, and a sinking into some level of consciousness beneath, or beside,

9. *New Yorker,* 5 April 1982, 193.
10. *The Tin Can Tree* (New York: Berkeley Books, 1983), 137.

language, where no tape of the preconscious is running. Yet, from the quiet of his study, uncannily accurate figures of life in its manifold freedom take form. Jeremy Pauling is an acknowledged portrait of the artist.

All of Tyler's protagonists share aspects of this style of consciousness, as it settles toward the passivity that enables them to become perceptive witnesses, authenticating by their presence the life around them. The dynamic of their thought is a slow jettisoning of the thingliness that attaches to an Updike protagonist, a ridding the self of what Charlotte Emory calls "Earthly Possessions." Charlotte, in the novel of that name, is Tyler's most thoroughly "Quaker" heroine. She is unworldly in an instinctive rather than a dogmatic way, and the voice inside her speaks of her capacity to witness and sustain others. As Charlotte sits in the passenger seat of Jake Simm's car, a hostage in his flight from a bank robbery, she makes a vivid contrast to Rabbit in his Toyota. When a passing parade in a small north Florida town interrupts their trip, Charlotte is required to witness a quarrel between Jake and his pregnant girlfriend, Mindy. In flight from her own family, and now in retreat from the makeshift family her kidnapping has thrust upon her, Charlotte, to filter out Jake and Mindy's troubles, watches the parade:

> The truth was that I was grieving for Jake and Mindy both, and I didn't know who I felt sadder for. I hate a situation where you can't say clearly that one person's right and one is wrong. I was cowardly; I chose to watch the parade. A team of Clydesdales clopped past with a beer wagon, and my eyes followed their billowing feet in a long restful journey of their own. The Clydesdales left great beehives of manure. I enjoyed noticing that. There are times when these little details can draw you on like spirals up a mountain, leading you miles.[11]

Rabbit, at forty-six, has turned from flight to acquisi-

11. *Earthly Possessions* (New York: Berkeley Books, 1984), 147.

tion, to getting "rich"—the natural extension of his spiritual predilection for the world, his terror at emptiness. There is an anxious sense of possession toward the objects his car-bound consciousness catalogs—*his* daughter, *his* chromosomes, *his* car stereo. Charlotte's alertness results from an opposite urge—an instinct to jettison. (A reverse kleptomaniac, she puts pieces of the family's furniture at the curb on trash days.) But to empty oneself, Charlotte learns, is merely to provide a cleaner slate on which the world will insist it be recorded. Resistance is futile, quiet is nearly unobtainable, but the pursuit of them characterizes perceptive people. Somehow, it is this scene that turns Charlotte homeward.

My Baltzellian parallels—Puritan Updike, Quaker Tyler—are useful, but admittedly imprecise. For, just as Updike started life a Pennsylvania Lutheran and got his Calvin from the New England climate, so Tyler began as a North Carolina Quaker—not a Philadelphian—and then became an undergraduate at Duke University, where she studied with Reynolds Price. In the process, Tyler picked up some regional peculiarities; next to its Quaker attributes, the second most visible element in her fiction is that "Southernness"—a problematic classification that, despite its ambiguity, cannot be ignored. As her Quaker inheritance has affected Tyler's rendering of consciousness, so her regional ties have helped her to define a sense of fictional event. On one Southern influence in particular Tyler is so emphatic and seems so correct that it leads her reader to break all the rules of modernism, to "trust the teller," to give credence to her self-observations.

All in all, Eudora Welty was a decidedly fortunate influence, and the courageous idiosyncrasy of her Southernness not only suggested how Tyler might write, but that she might write at all:

> I spent my adolescence planning to be an artist, not a writer. After all, books had to be about major events, and none had ever happened to me. All I knew were tobacco

workers, stringing the leaves I handed them and talking up a storm. Then I found a book of Eudora Welty's short stories in the high school library. She was writing about Edna Earle, who was so slow-witted she could sit all day just pondering how the tail of the C got through the loop of the L on the Coca-Cola sign. Why, I knew Edna Earle. You mean you could *write* about such people?[12]

In Welty, Tyler found a writer whose work provided manifold encouragement. Initially, there was this news that the familiar, the ordinary, was a rich field for cultivation, that a North Carolina town, or tobacco farm, would serve as a postage stamp of native soil. It was enough to get her started, and *If Morning Ever Comes* and *The Tin Can Tree*, for all their flaws, reveal a Weltian patience and pace, a willingness to build up texture from accurately observed details of gesture, speech, and object. Then, as Tyler's work matured through the 1970s, there was the gradual admixture of Welty's sharp-sighted yet compassionate eye and Tyler's Quaker sensibility.

In 1980, with the publication of Welty's *Collected Short Stories*, Tyler wrote an appreciation for the *Washington Star* that is perhaps her most important critical statement to date. In "The Fine, Full World of Welty," much of what Tyler says about the older writer is true of herself, especially her sense of the importance of character over plot. On the question of Welty's "Southernness," Tyler says:

Now: Is she, in fact, a Southern writer? (Someone will be bound to ask.) Well, assuming there is such a thing, I believe she qualifies—not only through accident of birth and her characters' rhythms of speech but also because, in telling a story, she concerns herself less with what happens than with whom it happens *to*, and where. Everything must have its history, every element of the plot its leisurely, rocking-chair-paced (but never dull) examination.[13]

12. "Still Just Writing," 14.
13. "The Fine, Full World of Welty," D1.

9

Tyler speaks of a world in which "events as preposterous as miracles float by on the flood of her words." And she distinguishes the "unkind events" in Welty's fiction from those in Flannery O'Connor's by finding in Weltian catastrophe "a sense that that's simply what happened; it's not the result of any willful twist from the author." This matter of authorial cruelty—the handling of violence and the grotesque—provides the reference point by which we can situate Tyler among her immediate Southern forebears.

Just as Eudora Welty has served Tyler as an intuitive model on the issue of causation, so Flannery O'Connor has provided her with an antitype. A Flannery O'Connor plot is a trajectory, a destiny that the protagonist resists with nightmarish futility. Yet religious irony is unremitting, bringing its quarry to ground. Consider young Tarwater in *The Violent Bear It Away*. Recalling the deed of drowning a retarded boy named Bishop, Tarwater acknowledges in spite of himself that he did perform the act to which his life was assigned, and that he said the words of baptism over the boy as he held him underwater. Here are the futile terms of his resistance to his fate:

> The fact that he had actually baptized the child disturbed him only intermittently and each time he thought of it, he reviewed its accidental nature. It was an accident and nothing more. He considered only that the boy was drowned and that he had done it, and that in the order of things, a drowning was a more important act than a few words spilled in the water. [14]

More even than its violence (a violence that we do sense as authorially inflicted), what Tyler resists in O'Connor's vision is the conviction of inexorability. From the accidental death of little Janie Rose in *The Tin Can Tree*, to the "suicide" of Timothy Emerson in *The Clock Winder*, to the

14. *The Violent Bear It Away*, in *Three By Flannery O'Connor* (New York: Signet NAL, 1955, 1983), 255.

10

random murder of Ethan Leary in *Accidental Tourist*, Tyler has written about people who occupy an accidental world, in which the fault for life's cataclysmic events is finally unascribable, and the duty of human beings is not to act but to endure, to define the degree of freedom possible within their confinement. As Serena Gill signals to Maggie Moran in *Breathing Lessons*, "We're not in the hands of fate after all . . . or if we are, we can wrest ourselves free anytime we care to."[15] To the best of her characters, Tyler has passed on her own attributes of silence, passivity, and compassion, along with a conviction that one must be prepared to confront a random and dangerous external world (one that is incomprehensible and therefore, for a novelist, unplottable) with an interior world that is empty, whitewashed, well swept, and alert for local discovery. Tyler's characters are not nearly so eccentric as reviewers tend to think. Rather, they possess that "extreme individualism" that Baltzell predicted of twentieth-century Quakers, faced with an absence of divine authority.

Thus, vestigial Quakerism and engagement in a peculiarly Southern debate conjoin to provide the central dynamic of Tyler's fiction, a shuttling of the imagination between inner and outer worlds, a series of impossible or at least impermanent choices. The mind retreats to an unworldliness that in a secular age has dwindled down to agoraphobia, or it goes anonymously adrift in the random. At one pole stands the phobic Jeremy Pauling of *Celestial Navigation*, leading almost no life at all. At the other stands the sociopath Morgan Gower of *Morgan's Passing*, trying to lead, in Tyler's phrase, "more than one life." Tyler's imagination, then, does not run on Updike's idea of "obsession." Instead, there is a haunting sense of dislocation. In response to it, one sits still, one breathes deeply. Or one travels. What is important is that Tyler imagines sane people who know that life is a trap, but that grace is a distinct possibility.

15. *Breathing Lessons* (New York: Alfred A. Knopf, 1988), 109.

The chapters that follow constitute readings of all Tyler's novels with the exception of *Morgan's Passing*, a book that possesses the symmetry of Tyler's best novels but links it to a psychology so abstract and implausible that the story drifts off its anchor. Chapter II examines Tyler's first three North Carolina novels. *If Morning Ever Comes* reveals Tyler's first success at identifying domesticity as her subject and dramatizes her youthful self-extrication from an onerous sense of Southernness, in which Faulknerian ideas of history prove an excessively demanding presence. *The Tin Can Tree*, as close as Tyler has come to minimalism, but without its deliberate truncation of sympathy, is Tyler's self-education in the pointillistic use of dialogue. Recorded regional speech offers only partial glimpses into a world of emotion that she acknowledges to be indeterminate. *A Slipping-Down Life*, which employs a colder eye than the previous book, verges on naturalism. It is the last book in which the limitedness of Tyler's characters constricts the emotional and narrative range of the fiction.

Chapter III examines the development of Tyler's pattern-building imagination in *The Clock Winder*. This novel initiates a "middle period" of novels, in which Tyler meticulously constructed dense, delicate, oriental-rug-like patterns of event and emotion over long spans of clock-measured time. The novels that cluster in this category are *The Clock Winder, Celestial Navigation*, and *Searching for Caleb*. There is a leisureliness to be seen in their stitchery that the earliest novels do not attain and the later ones eschew. Consideration of the Emerson family opens the inquiry into the role of agoraphobia in Tyler's design of character.

Chapter IV concerns *Celestial Navigation*. By examining narrative, by studying the shifting perspectives of the characters who constellate around Jeremy Pauling, the chapter explores the initial stages of Tyler's use of agoraphobia as artistic method. The mind in retreat forms the cornerstone of a theory of negative capability for Tyler, and I try to read *Celestial Navigation* as the poetics of that theory.

Chapter V, on *Searching for Caleb*, tentatively claims sociological referentiality for Tyler's sixth published novel, an expansion of her canvas outward toward the history from which she retreated in *If Morning Ever Comes*. But foremost is the genetic patterning that Tyler studies: her sense of her characters' need to establish identity in opposition to family myth and of the strange and beautiful symmetries their projects create.

Chapter VI pursues the chiastic rhetorical design of *Earthly Possessions*—a series of crossings of emotion, of fate, of longings—and establishes the psychiatric concept of "idealization" as central to Tyler's novels of the late 1970s. Idealization, the obsessive idea that only one's own home is singled out for unhappiness, is rich with fictive possibility. I argue that idealization—a longing gaze across the family fence—is the root of the double narration of *Earthly Possessions*.

Tyler's use of idealization comes to fruition in *Dinner at the Homesick Restaurant*. With her invention of Charlotte Emory's casual monologic voice, Tyler successfully abandoned the close density of presentation of the middle period, devising, as it were, a shorthand for her best effects. With *Dinner* she returns to the kaleidoscopic principle of those earlier novels—the study of a family as a set of intricate patterns turned through time. Yet she retains the capacity to surprise, to endow her characters with sudden insight, that marks the best work of the 1980s. Chapter VII also undertakes a study of Ezra and Cody Tull as embodiers of two philosophically opposed theories of the function of time in human experience.

Chapter VIII examines the roots of Tyler's depiction of the emotional shutting-down of Macon Leary in Freud's *Beyond the Pleasure Principle*. I try to read *The Accidental Tourist* as at once an intellectually rigorous and a wholly playful set of variations on Freud's theory of the death instinct. This chapter affirms Tyler's ability to benefit from a psychiatric approach to human pain and yet to remain free of the binding conceptual language, and the reduction of freedom, that systematic psychiatry implies.

Finally, Chapter IX is a consideration of *Breathing Lessons*, which is, despite its farcical elements, Tyler's most lyrical novel to date, a Keatsian contemplation of an autumnal landscape. Set in a single day, the book is an elaborate construction of mirrored anecdotes that together sum up the insights available to middle age. In Maggie Moran, Tyler offers a revision of her earlier opposition of phobic self and hazardous world. Measured breathing is a subtle and pervasive metaphor in the novel for the knowledge that we are not so much entrapped by the world as implicated in it. The mortality that gives significance to things lurks also within the self. Wisdom in *Breathing Lessons* lies in confronting the inevitable, as well as the accidental.

II NORTH CAROLINA NOVELS: *IF MORNING EVER COMES, THE TIN CAN TREE, A SLIPPING-DOWN LIFE*

TODAY, after twenty-five years of writing and with eleven published novels to her credit, Anne Tyler has traveled well past the point where the matter of her "Southernness" could inspire anxious self-questionings. Firmly defined as a novelist interested mainly in characters caught in the webs of time and domesticity, Tyler can confidently affirm and delimit the regional influence upon her fiction, point to Eudora Welty, and find there—for the appeasement of her curious readers—valid origins for her own leisurely pace and her habit of setting characters down in a highly colored, local world, with its capturable idiosyncrasies of speech.[1]

But in 1963, when she was twenty-two years old and at work on a first novel, such certitudes were not available. To be "Southern" might just as plausibly have meant to write like the South's other great practitioners— Poe, Faulkner, Flannery O'Connor, or even Carson McCullers. To read *If Morning Ever Comes* today, twenty-five years after its appearance, is to watch a young novelist backing into her abiding concerns and discovering the impertinence of the region's grander conceptions of "destiny." *If Morning Ever Comes* is undoubtedly a tentative performance taken alone (Tyler subsequently called it "bland");[2] but considered in the context of the

1. "I probably am the only writer who has written about Baltimore in a while, and it is wonderful territory for a writer. . . . And whatever it is that remains undeniably Southern in me has made it easy for me to switch to Baltimore. I lived four years in Canada and could write practically nothing about it at all." Quoted in Bruce Cook, "New Faces in Faulkner Country," *Saturday Review* 3 (4 September 1976): 40–41.

2. Clifford Ridley, "Anne Tyler: A Sense of Reticence Balanced by

books that follow, it offers glimpses of a writer's self-discovery.

Ben Joe Hawkes is a law student at Columbia University who hails from Sandhill, North Carolina, and keeps himself in a state of chronic anxiety about his family back home. Prior to the novel's opening, his father, Philip Hawkes, abandoned the family to move in with Lili Belle Mosely, a truly decent woman of lower social status. He has since died of a heart attack. A letter from Jennifer, the most businesslike of Ben Joe's six sisters, informs him that his oldest sister, Joanne, has left her husband in Kansas and returned to the family home with her baby, Carol. Joanne's return inspires Ben Joe to take a train south in order to combat an emotional waywardness in the family that he finds threatening. Once in Sandhill, he confronts the degree to which the women are happily independent of his support and protection. Idled by their indifference to his rescue attempt, Ben Joe visits his father's former mistress and decides to use some of the family savings to help her pay the bills for the hospitalization of young Philip, his father's illegitimate son, who has pneumonia. Joanne's husband, Gary, arrives and persuades her to go home with him. Ben Joe, out of nostalgia and a sense of personal irrelevance, proposes marriage to a sympathetic but insipid former girlfriend, Shelley Domer, and returns to New York with her in tow, "his own piece of Sandhill transplanted."[3]

In all Tyler's novels, the characters tend to be decent. In this first novel, though, that decency is downright egregious, as if characters and author alike were avoiding difficult scenes. For instance, young Philip, Ben Joe's illegitimate half-brother, an unresolved presence for Ben Joe, never appears at all. Gary arrives from Kansas and appears in the front hall just as his wife, Joanne, is about to leave on a date with Shelley Domer's boyfriend, and

---

'Oh, Well, Why not?'"

3. *If Morning Ever Comes* (New York: Berkeley Books, 1983), 265. Hereafter cited parenthetically in the text by page number.

Ben Joe walks away—taking the reader with him—rather than witness the altercation. Ben Joe's mother and paternal grandmother apparently have profound disagreements on the causes of Philip Hawkes's betrayal, but they never fight it out on the page. The only scene of any plot consequence actually narrated in the novel is Ben Joe's marriage proposal, and it is a lukewarm business at best, ending not in passion but with Shelley wrapping Ben Joe in a cocoonlike blanket.

On this rickety frame, Tyler hangs finely wrought moments—some of them promising, and some of them intriguing dead ends. For one, what is bumbled as drama succeeds in dream. Ben Joe is Tyler's first step toward the discovery of the gentle, agoraphobic male figure who will provide the center of vision for such fully realized novels as *Celestial Navigation* and *The Accidental Tourist*. If *Morning Ever Comes* is an experiment in the rendering of that remarkable consciousness, with its anxiety and humor, and Tyler presents Ben Joe's dreams startlingly well.

Actually, there is really only one dream—about his father—but it happens twice. As the title indicates, the novel's meditative subject is that irritable alertness that characterizes the consciousness in the hours before dawn. During his train ride south, and then again after a night of group insomnia at the Hawkes residence, Ben Joe dreams of his father, then dreams that his mother awakens him. She accuses him of dreaming of his father, he denies it, then he wakes for real.

The second instance of this nested dream is developed fully, consisting of two parts. The dream begins as a recollection of a story Ben Joe's father liked to tell about a trip to the Raleigh farmers' market with his uncle Jed. The men would arrive the night before and sleep on the ground. One night, a retarded boy named Quality Jones kept everyone awake by repeatedly asking his father the time. Then, when Quality fell asleep, his father repeatedly woke him to be sure he was all right. Uncle Jed rolled up his bag, said "Folks, if morning ever comes, I hope you get to meet this Quality," and went home. Half-awake, Ben Joe feels proud of the accuracy of his dream-work. Then the dream enters its second stage. He and his mother are on an unfamiliar porch, and an unknown old man is standing on the ground, reaching his hand up to Ben Joe:

> "Feel the *calluses*," the old man said. "I've worked and worked."
> "Don't do it," his mother said.
> He looked at his mother and then at the old man. He bent down toward the man's upturned, lined face and then he touched the man's hand, and quick as a wink the hand gripped his, vice-like, and hauled him off the porch and down to blackness.
> "*Mother!*" he screamed.
> But his mother's hand, reaching for him, gripped him harder, yanked him until his shoulder snapped. He was torn from the blackness back toward the porch but too far, and too hard, and now he was in greenness and falling even faster.
> "Wake up," a voice said.
> He awoke and he was on the glider, only it was the wrong color. In front of him stood his mother, looking out thought-fully across the lawn with her arms folded. When he opened his eyes the eyelids creaked and groaned and scraped like the heavy tops of old attic trunks, and at the sound his mother turned and glanced down at him.
> "You've been dreaming about your father," she said.
> "I haven't," said Ben Joe.
> "Ben Joe, *please*. Wake *up*."
> He opened his eyes for the second time; this time he knew without a doubt that he was really awake. At the foot of his bed stood his mother. (227–28)

This passage marks a beginning in Tyler's fiction; several elements here become important in the later novels. First, there is the metafictional theme of the doubling of the act of writing, the reproduction of the anxiety of the novelist in the insomniac fussiness of Ben Joe's dreamwork. He worries, and even interrupts his dream, when he realizes that he has cast his father as a young man but himself as an adult, an error in chronology. He stops the dream, then allows it to start again, like a film being edited. (This cinematic sense of time is a constant in Tyler's fiction; it becomes an explicit subject of *Dinner at the Homesick Restaurant*.) Also, Ben Joe wonders why the anecdote of Quality Jones is being told in his own anonymous dream-voice rather than in his father's voice. These are all novelistic concerns, playing upon the anxieties of the first novelist. In fact Tyler does make narrative mistakes—like having a minor character, Jamie Dower, come from both Connecticut and New Jersey and know who moved into a house in Sandhill, when he had neither been there nor known anyone from there for sixty years. Ben Joe's worrying over his houseful of women reproduces his author's worrying over her house of fiction, struggling to remember who is holding a teacup or a bowl of soup.[4] The doubling here initiates another sustained theme in Tyler's fiction: the perception that the work of the novelist is shared by her characters—that a sizable portion of the human enterprise is the act of bearing honest witness to the lives of others, an idea at the center of later novels such as *Searching for Caleb* and *Earthly Possessions*.

The second segment of Ben Joe's dream anticipates yet another dominant issue in later Tyler novels—that of emotional distance. The old man who seeks contact and sympathy is a representation of Ben Joe's dead—but once emotionally vital—father. His mother—who is characterized by others in the novel as a cold, icy Northerner—urges him to hold back. The dream opens Tyler's twenty-five-year inquiry into the subject of the proper space between people.

Finally, Ben Joe's dream composition has an agoraphobic shape, and it is agoraphobia that grips later Tyler heroes such as Jeremy Pauling in *Celestial Navigation* and

4. Twelve years later, Tyler's nocturnal composing was a less anxious affair. In 1976 she wrote that, at night, "some sort of automatic pilot works . . . to solve problems in my plots. I go to bed trustful that they'll be taken care of by morning. And towards dawn I often wake up and notice that my mind is still churning out stories without any help from me at all" ("Because I Want More than One Life," G7).

Macon Leary in *The Accidental Tourist*. For Ben Joe, the porch, with his mother present, represents a locus of safety that his father—who wandered into sexual transgression with a lower-class woman—threatens. Ben Joe finds himself yanked into blackness by the proffered hand. The imagery is recapitulated in Ben Joe's romantic picture of his family, a picture that the events of the novel are designed to correct:

> "I don't know why," he said. . . . "When I am away from Sandhill, sometimes the picture of it comes drifting toward me—just the picture of it, like some sunny little island that I have got to get back to. And there's my family. Most of the time I seem to see them sort of like a bunch of picnickers in a nineteenth century painting, sitting around in the grass with their picnic baskets and their pretty dresses and parasols, and floating past on that island. I think, I've got to get back."
> (199–200)

In Ben Joe, Tyler conjoins agoraphobia, anxiety about one's proper place in the family, and a compulsion toward insomniac storytelling. But while that conjunction anticipates later novels, other elements in *If Morning Ever Comes* do not. Both in the plot's initial design and in the relationships established there are vestiges of a kind of Southern fiction that an older Tyler knows she does not write. Certain decisions—like her emulation of Eudora Welty's mode of imagining and her avoidance of Flannery O'Connor's—were not final in 1963.

Consider the plot. A young man returns to his Southern hometown from his Northern university for two reasons. He has never resolved the meaning of his father's sexual waywardness, and he wants to prevent his sister's repetition of it. One has only to remember that Ben Joe was promised a Harvard education—denied him when his mother refused to accept the tuition money from a wandering husband—to sense that the Faulkner of *The Sound and the Fury* was as yet an unexorcised presence for the young Tyler. (There is another Faulknerian echo when

Ben Joe delivers support money for his father's illegitimate child in person to his father's mistress, recalling Ike McCaslin's visit to Fonsiba in *The Bear*.) *If Morning Ever Comes* reflects its author's early sense of obligation toward the grand Southern themes by taking up the temperamentally alien issue of inherited sexual guilt.

Furthermore—despite its tentativeness—there is a vestige of the Faulknerian theme of incest in Ben Joe's fixation on his sister Joanne.[5] His most frequently recalled memory is of Joanne in a red dress, with gold bangles on her arms and neck, flirtatiously meeting her "dates" at the front door. While ostensibly Ben Joe wants her to remain settled with Gary, the book hints at a Holden Caulfield–style chivalry in him, one whose terms do not bear examination. In fact, Ben Joe acknowledges that in high school he stopped seeing the patient and sympathetic Shelley Domer to start going out with girls who resembled Joanne. In spite of a certain sketchiness, Joanne is a sexually empowered character—a relative rarity in Tyler's fiction. Ben Joe's sense of her as an initiated big sister is among the best things in the book. But it is good for its subtlety and its accurate depiction of the ordinary. Quentin and Caddy Compson are behind it only as the faintest of traces, identifiable in Ben Joe's insomniac longing for his sisters to be asleep in their beds, not wandering in the night, beyond his control.

Another Southern trace—perhaps even fainter—is the Gothic of Poe. Tyler uses a house as the narrative center of the novel, surrounds it in Ben Joe's dreams with a ring of blackness, puts his beloved sister inside it in a red dress, and then keeps Ben Joe up all night in a state of nervous exhaustion. Like the house of Usher, the house of Hawkes is shown to have suffered deracination, as Ben Joe complains that traditional Southern roles have decayed:

A hundred years ago, maybe, you could look at a Carolina

5. Anne Jones, in "Home at Last and Homesick Again: The Ten novels of Anne Tyler," 3, calls it "a disturbing desire."

21

white man and know what he would have for supper that night, in what kind of house and with what sort of family sitting around him. But not any more—not in his case, at least. He felt suddenly pale and plain, going back to a big pale frame house that no one could tell was his. He looked at his reflection in the black windowpane and frowned, seeing only the flat planes of his cheeks and the worried hollows of his eyes. (26)[6]

Here Ben Joe's "pale" house dissolves into his own face, reflected in the window, a face that possesses "planes and hollows." Tyler uses the house as a projection of self, deftly blending architecture and physiognomy. Clearly, *If Morning Ever Comes* is not a novel of Gothic terror. Nevertheless, Tyler seems not yet to have delimited her Southern literary context. The substantial common element between Poe's story and Tyler's novel lies in the problematic status of the house in its narrator's mind. Poe's romantic point is that the mind's constructions are the embodiments of truth. Ben Joe must unlearn that lesson and see that time operates despite the mind's resistance. There exist both the actual unenchanted edifice and the romantic dream that nostalgia imposes. As he leaves alone for the train station, Ben Joe momentarily holds that difference firmly in mind (even as he reenacts the departure of Poe's narrator in "The Fall of the House of Usher"):

When he was across the street from his house he turned and looked back at it. It sat silently in the twilight, with the bay windows lit yellow by the lamps inside and the irregular little stained glass and rose windows glowing here and there against the vague white clapboards. When he was far away from home, and picturing what it looked like, this wasn't the way he saw it at all. He saw it as it had been when he was small—a giant of a place, with children playing on the sunlit

6. In an early interview with Jorie Lueloff, "Authoress Explains Why Women Dominate in South," Associated Press, *Baton Rouge Morning Advocate*, 8 February 1965, 11A, Tyler commented, "The most Southern thing about Ben Joe . . . is his inability to realize that time is changing."

lawn and yellow flowers growing in two straight lines along the walk. Now, as he looked at the house, he tried to make the real picture stay in his memory. If he remembered it only as it looked right now, would he miss it as much? He couldn't tell. He stood there for maybe five minutes, but he couldn't make the house register in his mind at all. It might be any house on the block. It might be anyone's. (255)

Ben Joe's fear of anonymity—here the anonymity of the New South—leads the novel into a consideration of race, an issue that Tyler's subsequent fiction largely ignores. It is as if the author of *If Morning Ever Comes* had not yet discovered that her imagination is most vividly engaged when circumscribed within private experience; that she will wear her Southernness lightly; that, as a writer who was born in Minnesota and transported to North Carolina, she did not inherit the consequences of slavery. *If Morning Ever Comes* opens with the premise that racial difference is the domain of the Southern novelist. But Ben Joe's thoughts on the black people in the train with him on his journey southward end at the Sandhill depot, and the novel's focus narrows to family for the duration.

Ben Joe's study of the black people on the train is a curious one. Given that the year is apparently 1962 or 1963, a time of racial turbulence in which a train such as this might well have carried freedom riders, it is strange that what Ben Joe reads in his fellow passengers is what Faulkner reads in Dilsey: tradition, stability, self-knowledge, a sense of one's place. All the virtues, in fact, that seem absent from his own family. The black men drink in the back of the car but return to their seats promptly when their wives demand it. (Unlike Ben Joe's wayward father.) The women talk of their eagerness for a Southern meal, and Ben Joe envies their firmly traditional sense of home. When they arrive at Sandhill, the blacks are met at the station by family, but Ben Joe has to walk home ungreeted. When he tells them about Joanne's baby, they are quietly shocked that his mother did not go to Kansas to help out.

Yet it is at the station that the novel gestures at addressing race—not as idealization, but in its virulent history. Here Tyler establishes the palimpsest motif essential to the novel's structure: "The waiting room was divided in two by a slender post, with half the room reserved for white people and the other half for Negroes. Since times had changed, the wooden letters saying 'White' and 'Colored' had been removed, but the letters had left cleaner places on the wall that spelled out the same words still" (39). This vestigial image suggests a great deal about the persistence of racism. Yet the novel moves swiftly inward, toward domestic matters, and never addresses the intriguing questions it raises. Does Ben Joe's chivalric attitude toward the women of his family rest on the Southern code? Does a young white man feel obligated to protect the innocence of his women because he subscribes to vestiges of the racial myth of the anarchic sexuality of the black male?[7]

Palimpsests recur in the book, and the sense of life as a layering of moments, of the past as a persistence, actually replaces the plot as the organizer of novelistic time. Ben Joe studies the family bulletin board in the kitchen and finds one of his own childish poems still hanging behind the messages of more recent years. He lies in his old room and archaeologically strips away layers of objects all the way back to the duck decals from his days as a toddler. Change, his sister Joanne teaches him, is to be accepted, and no real returns are possible—the family and one's place in it are never the same. Nostalgia falsifies.

There are, however, no black passengers on the journey north at the book's close, and the public, mythic dimensions of the Southern experience are stitches Tyler chose to drop. Whether Ben Joe's vision of Southern blacks was sentimental, or whether the deracination and insta-

7. See Anne G. Jones, *Tomorrow Is Another Day: The Woman Writer in the South, 1859–1936* (Baton Rouge: Louisiana State University Press, 1981), 3–50, for a discussion of the consequences of the code on women writers, consequences that Anne Tyler does not suffer.

bility he feels in his own family are historically limited to white Southerners, are questions that go unanswered. Tyler does not engage public historical issues again until she stretches the broader canvas of *Searching for Caleb*, and ultimately that book retreats from full sociological engagement as well. To frame this as an accusation is to blame Tyler for not being Tolstoy. But *If Morning Ever Comes* is interesting partly because, at twenty-two, she did not know she wasn't.[8]

On the other hand, familial aspects of the Southern myth do begin in *If Morning Ever Comes* and develop in the later works, and one in particular deserves consideration here. The Tyler myth, as the emergence of eleven novels allows it to be described, begins with an absconded father, a circumstance often established prior to the opening events of the novel. *If Morning Ever Comes* is the first instance of paternal abdication, and the terms of that act have not changed very much subsequently. Here is how Ben Joe describes his father's death to Joanne:

> "Two weeks before he died," Joanne said, "he was at home. I know he was. . . . Now, where was he when he died? Still at home?"
>
> "At Lili Belle's," Ben Joe said.
>
> "At—Oh." She shook her head. "Lately I've stopped thinking about her by her name," she said. "What with Gram calling her 'Another's House' all the time."
>
> "Well, he didn't *mean* to go and die there," said Ben Joe. "He'd been drinking a little, is all. Went out to get ice cubes and then forgot which home he was supposed to be going back to. Mom explained that to Lili Belle." (77)

Compare that to Amanda Pauling's account of the departure of her and Jeremy's father in *Celestial Navigation*:

> Our father was a building contractor who left us thirty-four

8. In "Because I Want More than One Life," Tyler wrote, "I am 34 years old now and see that I have a ceiling. There are limits to what I should attempt. At 22, I didn't know that yet."

years ago—went out for a breath of air one evening and never came back. Sent us a post card from New York City two weeks later: "I *said* I needed air, didn't I?"[9]

Or to Cody Tull's description of the departure of Beck Tull in *Dinner at the Homesick Restaurant:*

One weekend their father didn't come home, and he didn't come home the next weekend either, or the next. Or rather, one morning Cody woke up and saw that it had been a while since their father was around. He couldn't say that he had noticed from the start. His mother offered no excuses.[10]

The most recent version, and the least dramatic, is Ira Moran's father in *Breathing Lessons,* who waits until Ira finishes high school and then abdicates as head of the family picture-framing business to a chronic state of fabricated invalidism.

In *If Morning Ever Comes,* Tyler worked out her variant on the Southern myth of the evil patriarch. In Faulkner country, where slavery, incest, and rape have imposed a tragic vision of inherited guilt, Tyler's very first novel swerves away from an inherently Puritan vision toward the portrayal of fathers who are merely weak, never wicked. Tyler's abdicating fathers have nothing in common with King Lear; they always seem to act with an inadvertence that surprises even themselves. While it usually turns out that in some way they were stifled by the closeness of family life, they often are not able to articulate their position until years after their departure. Their unmalicious absence is a metaphor for the status of authority in the late Quaker sensibility.

The departure of fathers has consequences, but scarcely tragic ones. The family members endure, they go (to quote a short-story title) "foot-footing on." Ben Joe Hawkes's protectiveness, Amanda Pauling's envy, Cody Tull's icy

9. *Celestial Navigation* (New York: Berkeley Books, 1984), 25.
10. *Dinner at the Homesick Restaurant* (New York: Berkeley Books, 1983), 39.

efficiency, and Ira Moran's sardonic gaze are all unconscious responses to absent or abdicated fathers. But these
responses are never iron-clad; escape from the personality one's family imposes is always possible. *If Morning
Ever Comes,* with its tentative testing of Southern themes
public and private, its unraveling plot, and even its
dropped stitches, constituted a significant step on the
road to Tyler's mature comedy.

*   *   *

Anne Tyler's second novel, *The Tin Can Tree* (1965),
marks a narrowing of focus from *If Morning Ever Comes.*
The first novel reveals a young Tyler gravitating toward
the ordinary, nontragic aspects of human freedom—ambivalence, indecision, arbitrariness—despite her initial
commitment to a traditional "Southern" plot about sin
and its consequences. The reader watches her find a way
to examine private experience, in spite of the novel's large
communal backdrop. In *The Tin Can Tree,* Tyler pursues
the quietly unplottable element in human experience and
focuses on the private dimension.

In her critical writing, Tyler has occasionally addressed
this issue of the accidental aspect of experience and its
capturability by focusing on a small number of people in
a moment of time. Two instances provide an informal
definition of the aesthetic effect that she quite single-
mindedly pursues in *The Tin Can Tree.* In a 1976 review for
the *National Observer* of several photography books, Tyler
singled out a picture by the Czech photographer Joseph
Koudelka for its ability to haunt:

In one picture, a young man in handcuffs is standing in a
rutted farmyard. He looks stunned. From far behind, nearly
on the horizon, a row of black-garbed people watch him—
women in kerchiefs, men, children, a wary policeman, all
motionless. Well of course they're motionless; it's a photograph isn't it? But you have to remind yourself of that. It's
just *barely* a photograph. It's life on the page—so recently

suspended, so ready to start up again, that you have the feeling you've opened a door on somebody else's world by accident.

What more could you ask of any art?[11]

And here is Tyler on the sense of event in Eudora Welty's work:

> In Eudora Welty's small, full world, events float past as unexpectedly as furniture in a flood. A lady with her neck in a noose sails out of a tree; a stabbed woman folds in upon herself in silence; a child pushed off a diving board drops upright, seeming first to pause in the air before descending; a car rolls down an embankment, rocks in a net of grapevines, and arrives on the forest floor.
>
> All violent acts, come to think of it—but not at first glance. They are so closely observed, so meticulously described, that they appear eerily motionless, like a halted film.[12]

In these two passages, Tyler sets out some criteria for the kind of representation she has come to consider powerful, and toward which her fiction began to evolve in *The Tin Can Tree*. First, of course, a fiction must be a concatenation of persons and events that reveals no preordained significance, no imposed authorial agenda. It must surprise—first the author, then the audience. The Tyler character does not initiate an action, he responds to a predicament, and in a way that is, at its best, both unprecedented and recognizable. Second, a fiction must somehow mark its epiphanic status by seeming to suspend time. The taking of a photograph is an event in itself; inevitably, it intrudes upon the scene. When people see a camera, they pose, they hold still. For the right photographer, who intrudes minimally and promises to leave the dignity of his subject intact, such posing reveals more than it hides; it rescues from flux some essence of

11. "When the Camera Looks, It Looks for All of Us."
12. "The Fine, Full World of Welty," D_1.

the action it interrupts. And photography, as *The Tin Can Tree* demonstrates, is an apt metaphor for all acts of bearing witness, the writing of fiction chief among them.

In fact, *The Tin Can Tree* concerns a group of characters peering into one another's lives. They live in three segments of a long, tar-paper-roofed house outside the town of Larksville, North Carolina. Along the front porch are three front doors. The one on the right opens into the residence of James Pike, a handsome, twenty-eight-year-old photographer. James has left his home in Caraway, North Carolina, in an angry escape from a repressively religious father and has taken with him—out of guilt—his hypochondriac brother Ansel, who lies on their living room sofa and observes, with the keenly impertinent eye of the neurotic, the goings-on about him.

The door to the middle dwelling has two dead bolts and, since it is never open, no screen door. Behind it, in a maze of dressing screens, live the elderly Misses Faye and Lucy Potter, who temper their reclusiveness with an intense hunger for news of their neighbors.

The dwelling on the left is the home of the Pikes—the parents, their son Simon, and their twenty-six-year-old cousin Joan, who occupies a bedroom but never unpacks her suitcases, since life has trained her never to settle. The novel begins on a hill behind the house, at the conclusion of the funeral of the Pike's ten-year-old daughter, Janie Rose, who died when she fell from a tractor. Since the child's death, Mrs. Pike has retreated to her bedroom and ceased speaking. Instead of a conventional plot like the journey home in *If Morning Ever Comes,* we have the accident's aftermath—the actions and words of the house's survivors in the days following Janie Rose's death; the odd and asymmetric shakings-out of grief.

The walls of the house are thin. In the wee hours of a sleepless night, James can identify the nocturnal sounds not only of the Potters next door but even of Mr. Pike two doors away, who when he's had a few beers can be heard making ireful observations such as: "ninety-two point five percent of the people who live in the Southern states die of smothering." Miss Lucy Potter is an insomniac—a sympathetic one—and her slippers shuffle through the dreams of everybody in the house. When there's noise, or trouble, she taps on the walls with a thimble.

This house is radically different from the Hawkes place in *If Morning Ever Comes,* despite their shared status as anxious dream spaces. The Hawkes house was ancestral, and therefore a conventional Southern *mise-en-scène;* this house is zoned for multiple residency, with the peculiar gathering of residents an accident of real estate. The Hawkes house was gracious, upper middle class; here the grass is never cut, and there's a Model A on cinder blocks in the backyard. The Hawkes house held three generations, allowing Tyler to work out themes of inheritance; this one is ramshackle, and it resists any easy sense of "home."

As a book fascinated with the act of representation, it is fitting that *The Tin Can Tree* contains so many characters who are somehow versions of the artist. James takes pictures, Ansel makes speeches, Simon draws (Janie Rose used to), and the Potter sisters cut out silhouettes. Looked at together, they form an array of representational styles and stances and measure the extent to which one person can, through the exercise of skill, effectually alleviate the sorrow of another. Because of its initial premise of grief, the novel weighs all acts of representation in terms of their capacity to provide comfort.

The hypochondriac Ansel Pike, a compulsive monologuist, is the anti-artist of *The Tin Can Tree;* he is an exorcisable demon of misused language, everything Tyler wants drained out of her work. To an extent he resembles Ben Joe Hawkes: he maintains a program of surveillance, and he intrudes upon others ostensibly to help but with the underlying motive of keeping himself at the center of their attention. Ben Joe's intercourse was amiable; Ansel's is sniveling.

His hypochondria keeps him close to home, where he lounges on a sofa by the front porch window. This combination of agoraphobia and window gazing anticipates

30

Jeremy Pauling in *Celestial Navigation:* "He would sit on the couch with his elbows on the sill, and everything he saw passing—just an old truck, or a boy riding a mule—meant something to him. He had been watching that long, and he knew people that well."[13] One must wait for the later novel for an analysis of the paradox of the recluse who uncannily captures the nuanced motions of others' lives. Ansel's agoraphobia is merely a license to snoop for hidden motives. Nevertheless, thinking of Ansel as an anticipation of Jeremy provides one of the pleasures of the novel twenty years after its composition; it shows Tyler exploring numerous conditions—such as homesickness, agoraphobia, and accidentality—that she will raise to a conceptual level in later books.

Ansel specializes in shame. He says the things that can be lived with only as long as they remain unsaid. His rationale, as he explains it to James, is that he will die soon and he knows he will not be remembered for anything about his physical presence, so he must leave his words behind. Unlike the other characters who live in this house and maintain a powerful taciturnity, Ansel plans and then delivers formal speeches ostensibly meant to comfort his hearers. He begins, immediately after the funeral, by comforting young Simon, who flees the house and tells Joan, "I *hate* Ansel. I just *hate* him." Ansel intuits the emotional state of Mrs. Pike, who since Janie Rose's death has felt so guilty about her previous favoring of Simon that now she ignores him. Ansel's solution is to dress up and pay the formal visit to the Pikes that everyone has tried to dissuade him from making: " 'I just want to tell you,' Ansel shouted toward the kitchen, 'I know better than you can *imagine*, Mrs. Pike. You're just sorry now you weren't nicer to her, but I know how it feels to *really* miss someone' " (89). Ansel ferrets out a number of "shameful" secrets. He caught Janie Rose when her cigarette started the backyard on fire. He accuses James of the

13. *The Tin Can Tree* (New York: Berkeley Books, 1983), 18. Hereafter cited parenthetically in the text by page number.

unforgivable sin of continuing to despise their father. He spots Joan as she carries her suitcases to the bus in an aborted secret attempt to leave James forever, but keeps her secret for the sake of the moral blackmail it affords him. Yet his most vivid discovery involves a photograph that James took before Janie Rose died. "I'm ashamed of James," he says when he sees it:

> He pointed. His forefinger was just touching the Model A Ford that stood behind the house, resting on cinder-blocks that were hidden by the tall waving grass. All that could really be seen of the Ford was its glassless windows and its sunken roof—it had been submerged in that sea of grass a long time— and in the front window on the driver's side, no bigger than a little white button, was Janie Rose's moon-round face. She was too far away to have any expression, or even to have her spectacles show, but they could see the high tilt of her head as she eyed James and the two white dots of her hands on the steering wheel. She was pretending to be some haughty lady driving past. Yet when James drew back from the picture he lost her again immediately; she could have been one of the little patches of Queen Anne's lace that dotted the field. "I don't see how you found her," he told Ansel.
> "No trouble." (28–29)

The photograph proves—in the novel's inquiry into the subject of representation—to be the theoretical bone of contention between Ansel and James. Ansel does not like it because Janie Rose's presence in it is accidental. It is a casual incorporation of the dead, who deserve a degree of formality in all references to them.

In this scene, Ansel also examines two photographs James has taken of him. One shows him prone on the couch by the window, idle, playing with the blind cord. He prefers the other photograph, a formal portrait of himself sitting stiffly that he finds "heroic." Ansel insists that a portrait photograph be "a remaining thing"—a memorial that can outlast the living. This formality matches his manner of speech, which is premeditated, manipulative, and interminable.

At one point in the novel, Joan drifts off to sleep half-listening to Ansel fancifully describing his hometown for Simon, and she feels that she may drown in all the spilled words that come from him. But the story is also important. Ansel hates his home and yet makes Simon long to go there. It is the compulsive fictionalizing practiced by extreme recluses in other Tyler fictions, most particularly in the short story "The Bride in the Boatyard," published in *McCalls*, about a young girl who fabricates lives for herself and spins them out for strangers. Ansel's story of the town where boys wear earrings like pirates and all the citizens wear plumed hats precipitates Simon's running away from home, the act that ultimately restores Mrs. Pike to life, when she sees Simon's disappearance as a divine warning to continue loving those who are still alive.

James, who embodies the opposing vision of the artist, prefers the candid, informal, revealing side of photography that respects the dignity of its subject. James takes delight in the pointillistic representation of Janie Rose in the Model A because—as the book establishes—fragments are what are left of the dead; for that matter, fragments are largely what the living are able to communicate to, and make of, each other. James takes pictures that record people in acts and gestures that match his vision of them outside the moment of photographing them (that is, when he is not an intruding presence):

He had the idea of photographing everyone he knew in the way his mind pictured them when they weren't around. And the way people stuck in his memory was odd—they were doing something without looking at him, usually, wheeling a wheelbarrow up a hill or hunting under the dining room table for a spool of thread. . . . the pictures of people in his mind and in his filing cabinet were nearly identical. Joan he imagined in a dust storm, the way he had first seen her (she had come down the road with two suitcases and a drawstring handbag, spitting dust out of her mouth and turning her face sideways to the wind as she walked.) For a long time now he

33

had waited for another dust storm, and last week one had come. (23–24)

James's pictures are ambiguous. The dust around Joan replicates the hiddenness of Janie Rose. The viewer must labor to complete the picture. James's photographs also possess a feeling of time suspended. James waits for a second dust storm because it is a circumstance he does not impose but one that provides metaphorical power: Joan is not entirely knowable. It is significant that James's best picture to date—the elegy to Janie Rose and her comic cheekiness—was an accident. It marks Tyler's discovery that the detail happened upon is the source of the luminous; such details will constitute the building blocks, the pointillist's dots, of her fiction.[14]

As the valid artist figure, James is a reticent, silent presence in the book. He is an unobtrusive photographer, who must be coaxed at the Hammond family reunion to do a portrait of Aunt Hattie because her niece, Connie Hammond, thinks she is "fading." James finds this use of photography as a public memorial abhorrent, and he admires Aunt Hattie's feisty resistance to the reduction of herself to a two-dimensional, one-toned image. As James poses her, Aunt Hattie rebukes him for attempting to reduce the multiplicity of a human being to a flat, framed, formal, black-and-white image:

> Through the frame of his viewfinder he saw her standing just the way he wanted her, old-fashioned-looking and symmetrical, with her hands across her stomach and her mouth tight. Her face was like a turtle's face, long and droopy. It had the same hooded eyes and the same tenacious expression, as if she had lived for centuries and was certain of living much longer. Yet just in that instant, just as his hand tightened on

14. Gwendolyn Brooks noticed this aspect of *Tin Can Tree* in a short review for *Book Week* 3 (7 November 1965): 24. "The author, only 24, has a frugal, responsible hand. Her frugality is selective—and kind to us, because the spaces are for us to fill. We are aides in the mixed work of creation."

the camera and his eyes relaxed at seeing the picture the way
he had planned it, something else swam into his mind. He
thought of Miss Hattie coughing, in the center of the family
reunion—not defiant then but very soft and mumbling, telling them all she was sorry. He frowned and raised his head.

"Well?" said Miss Hattie.

"Nothing," James said. (72)

James's taciturnity connects his speech to his photography. A dialogue between him and Ansel points up their
opposition. Ansel is speaking about his homesickness, a
feeling he seems to have fabricated for the purpose of
conversation:

"I'm going back there sometime," he was saying. "They'll
forget, and I'll go back. I crave a religious atmosphere." He
lay back down and James nodded to himself, thinking maybe
he would be sleepy now. "Churches here are somewhat
lacking, I think," Ansel went on. "Quiet-like. At home it was
better. Mrs. Crowley spoke in tongues. There was things
bound you there. A red glass on the windowsill in the choir
loft, with something brown rising above it like the head of a
beer. I think now it was wax, and the glass was a sort of
candle. But before I thought it was a sort of brown fungus,
some kind of mold just growing and growing. Do you remember, James?" He waited a minute. "*James?*" he said, and
now his voice rose even above the roaring of the rain.

"No, I don't," James said.

"Sometimes I think your mind is just a clean, clean slate,
James."

"I keep it that way," said James. (136–37)

As a result of James's preference for blankness, his feelings in the novel are in fact left for the reader to supply.
When Tyler supplies a reason for James's burdening himself with this hypochondriac brother, and thus sacrificing
his chance to marry Joan, her narrator is as reticent as
James himself.

If Joan were to go, he had only two choices. That was the
way he saw it. He could let her be, and spend the next forty

years remembering nothing but the way she used to walk across the fields with him from the tobacco barns and the peppermint smell of her breath when she kissed him good night. Or he could go after her and say, "Come back. And will you marry me?" In his *mind* he could say that, but not in real life. In real life he had Ansel, and would have him always because he couldn't walk out on that one, final member of his family that he hadn't yet deserted. (175–76)

When held against the scene in which James and Joan walk home from tying tobacco, with the wind drying the sweat on Joan's back and the tobacco gum on her hands and between her toes, this explanation is unsatisfactory. While Joan is an erotically realized character, James's compulsion is insufficiently explained. It is one space in the novel the reader cannot fill. James's inability to live—in spite of his palpable vitality—remains a troubling mystery.

The novel does suggest its probable consequences, however. James and Ansel tend to wear each other's clothes—James in Ansel's pajamas; Ansel in James's red shirt. This is a trait they share with the Potter sisters, who take turns wearing the family pendant watch. The whole house is a gallery of agoraphobes, but its two severest seem to stand as a warning that their shared loneliness is James's future if he does not shake Ansel. The Potter sisters' art form is the silhouette. As a party game, they cast a light on a friend's profile and trace a shadow on paper taped to the wall. They have also built a life-size silhouette of a man reading, which they place in their front window in order to scare off burglars. They have made so many silhouettes of the house's residents that now everyone has a silhouette of everyone else—a metaphor for the limitations to what can ever be known concerning another human being. At the book's conclusion, when Mrs. Pike and James have returned with Simon and Joan has come home from her own attempt to run away, the Misses Potter make silhouettes at an impromptu party. James offers to photograph them at their work. The others want James in the picture, so it is finally Joan who snaps the shutter:

In the finder of the camera Joan could see them moving, each person making his own set of motions. But the glass of the finder seemed to hold them there, like figures in a snowflurry paperweight who would still be in their set positions when the snow settled down again. She thought whole years could pass, they could be born and die, they could leave and return, they could marry or live out their separate lives alone, and nothing in this finder would change. They were going to stay this way, she and all the rest of them, not because of anyone else but because it was what they had chosen, what they would keep a strong tight hold of. James bent over Ansel; Mrs. Pike touched the top of Simon's head, and Mr. Pike sat smiling awkwardly into space. "It starts near the arches," said Ansel, "right about here . . ."

"Be still," said Joan.

She kept her head down and stared at the camera, smiling as if it were she herself being photographed. The others smiled back, each person motionless, each clutching separately his glass of wine. (269–70)

The book ends with Tyler's ideal photograph—a slowing to a moment of suspension, a flash of captured gestures. As with James's picture of Aunt Hattie, it is in the fleeting second just before everyone grows still for the formal pose that each person's reality is manifest. A second later, the camera gets only a trace of that reality, in which character is revealed in an accuracy that action cannot contradict, where everyone is shown to be both free and frozen.

Pointillism is the central technique, as well as a central subject, of *The Tin Can Tree*. What is distinctively new in this book is its dialogue—musically rendered, inconclusive, and comic in its apparent insufficiency as a mode of human communication. The novel's conversations establish a thin surface of banality beneath which seismic emotions lurk. More is heard in its silences, gaps, misunderstandings, and failures to listen than in the words themselves. In this it seems to approach, albeit for gentler purposes, the language of Harold Pinter or David Mamet.

It is a brilliant stroke to premise the book on a death in the house—a time when people feel obligated to speak—and then to create characters of such astounding taciturnity. Several words and phrases, always at the beginnings of sentences that never get spoken, form the actual dots of Tyler's pointillism. Characters say "Oh," "Well," "*Oh*, now," and then they stop. The consequence is anxious, even rueful comedy. After an inconclusive quarrel with Joan, James even notices how people in this book talk:

> Simon shrugged and sat down on the couch. Now that they were all seated here, facing each other and keeping their hands folded in their laps, it seemed more awkward than before. It seemed they should be having a *conversation* of some kind, something that made sense. Not these little jagged bits of words. He tried smiling at Joan but all she did was smile back, using only her mouth while her eyes stayed serious and maybe even angry; he didn't know. "Would you rather I come back another time?" he asked.
> "It's all right."
> "Well." (179–80)

When James returns to his family home in Caraway, in search of the runaway Simon, he confronts the father he has not seen in three years. They have nothing left in common but their taciturnity:

> He had to look down to the level of his shoulders, much lower than he had remembered, into the old man's small lined face and his eyes in their pockets of bone. His hair was all white now, gleamingly clean. He wore suspenders, snapped over a frayed white collarless shirt which was only folded shut, without buttons. And his trousers bagged at the knees.
> "The dog didn't bark," said James.
> "She died," his father said, and stepped back a step to let him into the house. (242–43)

The reunion of the rejected Simon and his emotionally stunned mother is the novel's climax, yet it eschews all eloquence. Mrs. Pike reclaims Simon and herself for the future in the following way:

> James suddenly thought, what if he *won't* come back? The same idea must have hit Mrs. Pike. She said, "Don't you *want* to come?"
>
> "Well," Simon said.
>
> "You can't stay *here*."
>
> "How did you happen to come by?" he asked.
>
> "James thought of it."
>
> "I mean, what for? Did you just go off driving?"
>
> Mrs. Pike frowned at him, not understanding. "James thought of it," she said. "He thought you'd be in Caraway."
>
> "You mean you came specially?"
>
> "Well, *yes*," said Mrs. Pike. "What did you think?"
>
> "*Oh*," Simon said, and the sudden clear look that came across his face made James feel light inside and relieved. (246–47)

Such misunderstandings are the staple of the novel's dialogue, yet these characters never appear stupid. The limited omniscient form of narration provides a very circumscribed account of the characters' thoughts, but it keeps largely to their visual experience and never ventures toward profundity.

In only one scene is this principle of ineloquence waived, and then only for a moment. When James and Joan go to work for a day harvesting and tying tobacco, the women who do the tying discuss Mrs. Pike's retreat from life. The scene is a set piece, a vignette of labor, modestly reminiscent of Levin's wheat harvest in *Anna Karenina*. An immense and vital black woman named Missouri moves and halts through lapses of memory and changes of subject to the one inclusively valid statement in the book. The pointillistic dialogue is richly comic but too long to quote more than its conclusion:

> "That boy of theirs. You know him, Joan?"
>
> "He's my cousin," said Joan.

"Oh, yes. Yes. Simon. Going to go to pieces if things go on this way. Do you see what I'm getting at?"

"Well, no."

"It's as plain as the nose on—Boy? Come on, now, quit that poking. I'm saying it's Simon should be in her beauty shop with her."

"In her—?"

"I mean in her sewing shop. Look what you done now, got me all confused. Well, that's who you want."

"You mean he should entertain the customers," Joan said.

"That was my point."

"Well—"

"He's the only one who can help now. Not hot tea, not people circling round. Not even her own husband. Just her little boy."

"I don't see how," said Joan.

Missouri made an exasperated face. "*You* don't know," she told her. "You don't know how it would work out. Bravest thing about people, Miss Joan, is how they go on loving mortal beings after finding out there's such a thing as dying. Do I have to tell you that?" (105–6)

Like the blacks in *If Morning Ever Comes*, Missouri is given wisdom and comments chorically on the white people around her. But the inadvertence of her insight marks her as a genuine citizen of the novel. What Tyler has taught herself in *The Tin Can Tree* she makes use of in subsequent works; it is a realism of found language, a way of coaxing the reader to identify and trace patterns of the heart's truth in the pointillistic dialogue of her characters.

*   *   *

That inarticulateness of character becomes the dominant aspect of Anne Tyler's third novel, *A Slipping-Down Life*, which had its imaginative beginnings in a news clipping about a fifteen-year-old Texas girl who slashed "Elvis" on her forehead. Tyler's shortest book, it appeared in a considerably condensed version in *Redbook* before being published by Knopf later the same year.

Because of the narrowness of its Southern, small-town setting, the underripeness of its adolescent protagonists, and the deadpan reportage of its narrative voice, *A Slipping-Down Life* qualifies as minimalist fiction. Tyler has observed that it was the second novel that she tried to write "mostly at night,"[15] in consequence of the birth of her children, and the novel does seem to operate on the principle of conserving authorial energy. The characters are self-absorbed in the manner of people usually found in naturalistic fiction, robotically pursuing ends that strike the reader as ill-defined, grotesque, and self-destructive. They do not so much live their lives as get enmired in them, and they struggle with the leaden awkwardness of terrapins to get free. The major narrative effort of the novel is to keep to its flatness and avoid any conspiratorial wink at the reader. "Such people exist in multitudes" the narrator implies, "and *I* find nothing surprising about them." It is thus not an absence of sympathy that causes the book to run against the grain of Tyler's other fiction but rather that its sympathy is so very arch. Most uncharacteristic of all is the protagonists' utter incapacity to experience those moments of strabismal insight—the seeing of things "on a slant"—that is the identifying trait of the leading citizens of Tyler's first two books and, of course, of all those from *The Clock Winder* on.[16] Were it not for its sympathy, *A Slipping-Down Life* could be mistaken for a Joyce Carol Oates novel.

The novel concerns a year in the life of Evie Decker, a lumpily unattractive seventeen-year-old who hears an

15. Stella Nesanovich, "The Individual in the Family: A Critical Introduction to the Novels of Anne Tyler," xxi. The first nocturnally composed novel, *Winter Birds, Winter Apples,* was never published.

16. There is one exception. The Deckers' black maid, Clotelia, picks up some of Missouri's choral function and is the only character in the novel capable of real verbal vividness. Tyler has prevented any risk of sentimentalizing blacks here by making Clotelia politically radical, only marginally supportive, and a very bad housekeeper. For another, equally vital version of Clotelia, see the short story "The Geologist's Maid," *New Yorker,* 28 July 1975, 29–33.

interview on the radio with a local rock singer named Bertram "Drumstrings" Casey. Evie starts catching Casey's act at a local roadhouse. Then, on a particularly raucous night, she comes out of the ladies' room with his last name carved distortedly into her forehead. The event catches Casey's attention, and, in dutiful pursuit of "Publicity," he takes along a newspaper photographer to visit her in the hospital. Their conversation has the sense of inadvertence and the crossing of lonely purposes that characterizes all the novel's relationships, including the eventual, short-lived marriage of Drum and Evie:

> "What'd you go and cut it backwards for?" he asked her.
>
> "It just worked out that way," said Evie.
>
> "Worked out that way, how do you mean?"
>
> "I don't know, that's just the way it happened. Can't you read it?"
>
> "Sure, I can read it."
>
> "Now I can see that it's uneven," Evie said.
>
> "I know that's going to bother me. Every time I look in a mirror I'll think, why did I let the Y droop. Why did I shake on the C?"
>
> "Why did you make it 'Casey'?" Casey said.
>
> She stared, mistaking his meaning. She thought he had asked the only question she minded answering.
>
> "Why not my first name?" He asked. "There're thousands of Caseys around."
>
> "What, *Drumstrings?* I don't have that big of a forehead."
>
> "Drum," he said. "Nobody says the whole thing, for Lord's sake."[17]

Drum's icy self-absorption has its fascination, and certain aspects of it anticipate the evasiveness of Tyler's more developed artist figures, such as Jeremy Pauling in *Celestial Navigation*. In a 1972 interview for the *National Observer,* Tyler said that it was Drum's character that made her fond of *A Slipping-Down Life:* "Yes, it's a different kind

---

17. *A Slipping-Down Life* (New York: Berkeley Books, 1983), 54–55. Hereafter cited parenthetically in the text by page number.

of book; I felt as I was writing it that I was being braver. *If Morning Ever Comes* and *The Tin Can Tree* were so much alike; I think I'd gotten tired of my own voice. . . . I still like the book. I love Drumstrings Casey, his family, everything about him. He's the direct inheritance of all the days on the tobacco farm."[18]

Certainly, Drum is the first in a series of exciting, anarchic, and even amoral young men in Tyler's fiction. In every case, they are poor, white, and live in North Carolina.[19] But where Guy Tell (Mary Tell's first husband in *Celestial Navigation*) appears through an erotically charged memory of his bony back and his spandex bathing suit, Drum—despite numerous opportunities in scenes at the Unicorn roadhouse—never attains any physical immediacy. Evie Decker, the novel's center of consciousness, just does not wake up sufficiently to register his sexiness for the reader, who ends up having to take her word for it. During his songs, Drum stops to "speak out" in nonsequential fragments. They excite Evie, and she says to her friend Violet: "It made me want to answer. You know those girls who scream on the Ed Sullivan show? Well, now I know why they do it" (18).

Drum's glossolalia during his songs is part of a motif concerning language in the novel. Repeatedly, Tyler metaphorizes language as a web. To allow oneself to be named, or marked, in the book's system of signification is to become entrapped. Drum's deepest urge is to get away

18. Clifford Ridley, "Anne Tyler: A Sense of Reticence Balanced by 'Oh, Well, Why Not?'": 23. If Evie had stood in front of a mirror and carved "drum," she would have infelicitously ended up with MUЯD on her forehead.

19. One of the most engaging is Eugene Bennet, the boy who disrupts the reform school graduation in "The Genuine Fur Eyelashes," *Mademoiselle* 69 (January 1967): 102-3, 136-38. Like Drum, Eugene comes from a family of towheads who all turn dark-haired in adolescence. Another is Jonas, who invents a funeral ritual for the ashes of his uncle "Wurssun" in "Dry Water," *Southern Review* 1 (April 1965): 259-91. There is Southern grotesquery in these stories, and their voice is akin to that of *A Slipping-Down Life,* but the characters are truly comical in their stolidity. In them, Tyler's deadpan serves laughter rather than archness.

from Pulqua, North Carolina, and never to return. This longing for unencumbrance is expressed in his words. The "speaking out" he performs in his songs is random, and his questions, until the novel's final scene, permit no meaningful verbal response. Offstage, Drum will not engage in conversation; whenever possible, he answers only in concrete terms and only when asked a direct question. He will not talk about emotion.

Yet his taciturnity does not prevent marriage to Evie Decker. Drum's manager and drummer, David Elliot, attempts various stunts to get Drum publicity, and Drum, who is superstitious about his own success, despises David's efforts because they define him. Thus, at first, Evie's mutilation is disturbing to Drum, and he admits that her presence gives him a sinking feeling. David hires her to sit and stare at Drum during performances. The publicity temporarily boosts Drum's career, but Evie's presence in the bar fills him with guilt and a sense of encumbrance. When he announces at a tent revival (where they have gone to pull a publicity stunt) that he finds Evie unattractive, she abandons him, his "luck" goes bad, and he proposes marriage in an attempt to reverse the direction of his "slipping-down life." Marrying the girl on whose forehead his name is already carved is acceptable to Drum because Evie is not so much another human being as a talisman.

As Drum sinks into listlessness and failure, Evie takes up David's game and dreams up a stunt. She hires several girls to kidnap Drum from the tar-paper house where she and Drum have taken up married life. They will hide him in David's toolshed while Evie notifies the police and the newspapers. But as this stunt is in mid-execution, Mr. Harrison, her school principal, comes to tell her that her father is dying of a heart attack. She arrives at the hospital to find him already dead.

When she returns to the tar-paper house the next morning, Drum is in bed with Fay Jean Lindsay. But what angers Evie is that he will not move back to her family house. She tells him she is pregnant; when it makes no difference, she goes home, changed from her year of Drum Casey, a wiser and more self-directed young woman.

The final scene is in the Unicorn, where Drum "speaks out" of one of his rock songs:

> *"Where is the circular stairs?"* he asked.
> And then, *"But the letters was cut backwards."*
> *"Would you explain?"*
> His audience just nodded, accepting what he said. The only person who could have answered him was not present. (221–22)

There does appear to be a mystery here. Comments on the novel I have read invariably state that *A Slipping-Down Life* is about a girl who cuts a rock singer's name in her forehead. Yet, in the hospital passage I quoted, Evie feared that Drum had asked "the only question she minded answering." And when she and Drum break up, she tells him:

> "I didn't cut my forehead. Someone else did."
> "You don't make sense," Drum told her.
> "Well, you were there. You remember how it was. The singing was good and there were fans shouting back at you and lots of people dancing. When I went into the restroom an argument started up. I forget just how. Me and a redhead and some friend of hers. She got mad. She told her friend to hold me down and she slashed your name on my face. 'I hope you're satisfied,' she said. *That* was how it happened." (220)

Thus, the question Drum asks no one in particular is, *Why, if it wasn't done in a mirror, were the letters cut backward?* When the condensed version of the book was published in *Redbook*, it was accompanied by an illustration, a pen-and-ink drawing of a rather cherubic Evie with the letters ⅄Ⅎ⅂ᴧ⋋ on her forehead. These are clearly the mirror reverse of the word, precisely what Evie would have cut standing in front of a mirror. The letters do not appear again in the *Redbook* text. In addition, the *Redbook* version of a key passage differs from the full-length version. The *Redbook* version reads: "She had cut the letters with a pair

45

of nail scissors. They ran all the way across her forehead, large and ragged and Greek-looking because straight lines were easier to cut: the letters themselves were backward." In the full-length version (the opening of chapter 4, on page 39), the letters actually appear. The passage reads: "She had cut the letters with a pair of nail scissors. They ran all the way across her forehead, large and ragged and Greek-looking because straight lines were easier to cut: ⊂ⱱƧƐλ ." Tyler removed the sentence "The letters themselves were backward." Here the order of the letters is *not* reversed, but correct. However, the S is facing the wrong way; the A and the Y are upside down; and the C and E would appear the same inverted or not. If the redhead had knelt above Evie's head and attempted to carve the letters so they would appear in the correct order but forgot to invert them, this is what she would have carved.

Apparently Evie, responsive to the sexual significance of Drum's "speaking out," was embroiled in a competition over him in the ladies' room and ended up marked with his name. (A naturalistic allegory of adolescence and marriage.) Or, in a more sinister reading, David put the redhead up to it as another publicity stunt. David's edginess and Drum's guilt provide considerable inconclusive evidence for that reading in the novel.

In either case, yet another look at that key passage in the full-length version reveals that Tyler has slipped in unreliability among the other vices of her narrator. Here is how she inscribes the facts of Evie's scars:

> She had cut the letters with a pair of nail scissors. They ran all the way across her forehead, large and ragged and Greek-looking because straight lines were easier to cut: ⊂ⱱƧƐλ . In the emergency room, after they had swabbed the blood away, there was a silence lasting several seconds. "*Backwards?*" someone said finally. It looked as if she were staring out at the letters from within, from the wrong side of her forehead. Or maybe she had cut them while facing a mirror. Whatever the reason, Evie wasn't telling. (39)

And neither is her author. At least not here.

A pleasing paradox results from the awareness that Evie did not do it: Evie found her way to an identity as an adult and as a mother, heir to the family house, and a survivor of the *anomie* and anonymity of adolescence, through the consequences of an event that was not her choice but accidental. Ironically, when she is in the hospital she tells Violet, "While I was walking through that crowd with the policeman, I kept thinking of my name: Evie Decker, *me*. Taking something into my own hands for once. I thought, If I had started acting like this a long time ago my whole *life* might've been different" (43). While she did not do the carving, it was her name that Evie learned. Drum says as much, inadvertently, when Evie leaves him: "Now that you have done all that cutting . . . and endured through bleeding and police cars and stitches, are you going to say it was just for purposes of *identification?*" (219–20). The adolescents in this novel suffer from a kind of moral *dysgraphia;* in their attempts to learn to write their own names (self-assertion as a "publicity stunt"), they get things backward at first, but at least it is a beginning. Somewhere underneath these word-games lies a theory that explains the randomness, the accidentality, of adolescent behavior. Young human beings have to initiate or suffer some action—however purposeless—in order to be buffeted toward identity. If a reader can stretch his imagination just enough to take adolescents and adolescent fiction seriously, *A Slipping-Down Life* begins to resemble Poe's "A Purloined Letter." It can be pleasurable to be tricked. But on second thought, it is just as well Tyler gave this game up.

III *THE CLOCK WINDER*

WITH *The Clock Winder,* the texture of felt experience in Anne Tyler's fiction achieved a new complexity. Having quickly abandoned the Southern Gothic device of constituting the past as a single, originating event—the "sin" of Philip Hawkes in *If Morning Ever Comes*—the novelist formulated a technique for representing the past's persistence in the patterns of thought, speech, and behavior of members of a family. In *The Clock Winder,* Tyler looks at the life of a family in a series of cross sections, where the past lingers as a set of propensities, even quirks, rather than as a story. As the Emersons develop into a set of psychological variations on the theme of emotional dependency, the sense of their common past takes shape as a series of innumerable events, half-forgotten in their specifics, laid over one another across the decades. Selfhood is defined as a palimpsest; the earliest and most formative events may well be unrecoverable, yet their effects are palpable in the peculiar topography of any character's present anxieties, enthusiasms, even habits of speech.

The consequence of this advance in realist technique, and its gain in psychological accuracy, is a relativistic presentation of those events that do get remembered. Henceforth in Tyler's fiction, instead of an unequivocal past that holds a determining act, there is only the disagreed-upon family anecdote, whose meaning each member has interpreted differently, self-interestedly, responsibility for which is finally indeterminate.

From *The Clock Winder* on, the typical Tyler character is forever engaged in writing his own autobiography, composing apologias for attitudes and gestures that are deeply ingrained, irretrievable in origin, and often a little compulsive. The Tyler character will react in a way that fits his or her individual pattern, although the overt consequences may prove utterly unpredictable or paradoxical. Which response you get depends on how deeply you scratch—or wound—a character. For instance, in *The Clock Winder* there is Billie Emerson, the dead father of the Emersons, whose former solicitude and subsequent absence have stamped rich patterns of incompetence on his widow and offspring. There was something a little vulgar about Billie's ability to make money, something déclassé that does not afflict his fey survivors, something that serves as the humiliating entrée to his layered self:

He mourned for weeks when Mary refused to be a debutante, and he joined the country club on his own and played golf every Sunday although he hated it. "What do I go there for?" he asked. "What do I want with those snobs?" He was made up of layers you could peel off like onion skins, each of them equally present and real. The innermost layer (garage mechanic's son, dreaming of a purple Cadillac) could pop up at any time.[1]

Tyler ensures that even this economic analysis of Billie Emerson is not the central layer of the onion. The passage is narrated as free indirect discourse: the reader is hearing *Matthew's* rehearsal of the family's consensus version of their father, and Matthew, who is not good with money, has a vested interest in its validity.

Distrust of the central layer, the bottom line, is habitual in Tyler's thinking. In a 1978 review of Julian Symons's *The Tell-Tale Heart: The Life and Works of Edgar Allan Poe,* she wrote of Symons's presentation of Poe that "the effect is one of layers—of the levels of knowledge through which we proceed in getting to know any living person."[2] She distinguished four layers in Poe: the aristocratic dandy, the addict, the imaginer, and finally the psychiatric subject. She concluded: "In fact, it is [the] . . . third layer that is most revealing. The fourth, innermost layer—the Freud-

1. *The Clock Winder* (New York: Berkeley Books, 1983), 108. Hereafter cited parenthetically in the text by page number.
2. "The Poe Perplex."

ians' interpretations of Poe as sado-necrophilist, the critics' elaborate constructions of his symbols and allegories—seems beside the point. As Symons himself says, these theories do not so much explain as explain away."

In her sense of the self, Tyler has one conviction in common with Lacanian theory—that at center the self is unstable and constituted by linguistic patterns. The pointillism of the dialogue in *The Tin Can Tree*—its digital patterning of speech—is put to rich psychological use in *The Clock Winder* as Matthew thinks of his mother's voice as the closest thing to the family's core:

> In this sunporch, where the family had always gathered, Mrs. Emerson's long-ago voice rang and echoed. "Children? I mean it now. *Children!* Where is your father? When will you be back? I have a right to know your whereabouts, every mother does. Have you finished what I told you? Do you see what you've done?" On Timothy's old oscilloscope, she would have made peaks and valleys while her children were mere ripples, always trying to match up to her, never succeeding. Melissa was a stretch of rick-rack; Andrew's giggles were tiny sparks that flew across the screen. Margaret only turned the pages of her books and tore the corners off them. She was a low curved line, but Matthew was even lower—the EKG of a dying patient. He pulled the afghan up closer around him. (229–30)

Tyler's distaste for the arrogance of psychiatry's claim to provide final explanations and her delineation of the self as a shifting but persistent pattern combine to shed light on her artistic exploration of agoraphobia. The Emersons—and Elizabeth Abbot, their "handyman"—are beings who are ultimately mysterious, but whose psyches are organized around pronounced patterns of fear and avoidance.

Both by definition and in this novel, the term *agoraphobia* applies to a spectrum of responses, at one extreme a crippling obsessional neurosis, at the other a philosophical preference for a private life. In *The Clock Winder*, "agoraphobia" operates predominantly at the self-conscious end of the spectrum. With the exception of Andrew

Emerson (who is clinically disturbed), Tyler's characters have sculpted a rhetorical and philosophical stance, a style of being, out of their compulsions. Elizabeth Abbot, for instance, shapes her anxiety into a personal art of comic inconsequence. In this novel's imagining, agoraphobia possesses a dialectical quality, a dynamic. It is as much a hall of mirrors, as capable of paradox, as is Kierkegaard's concept of dread or despair. In other words, it becomes an intellectual construction, a romantic idea. It, and not mere empirical observation of middle-Atlantic, middle-class Americans, orders the invention of character in the novel.

The psychiatric literature on agoraphobia has traditionally attributed considerable complexity to the syndrome. As an inheritor of Hegel, Freud built a dialectical movement into the defense mechanisms; the paradoxical qualities of projection and reaction-formation characterize his description of the phobias. In his famous "Analysis of a Phobia in a Five-Year-Old Boy,"[3] Freud concluded that little Hans's terror of going into the street centered on an irrational fear of horses. Little Hans associated the male sexuality of these animals with the father toward whom he felt Oedipal aggression; this repressed aggression returned first as anxiety and finally as compulsive fear. Freud's discovery of aggression as the source of fear was replicated in the work on female agoraphobia subsequently done by Helene Deutsch, in which fear of public places was discovered to be an expression of an unconscious desire for, and anxiety about, the loss of sexual control.[4] While psychoanalysis offers suggestions to the novelist for constructing a supreme fiction from the idea of agoraphobia, it does, of course, invariably tie that fiction to a final explanation in the Oedipus complex. Tyler has wisely cut her subject adrift from any moorings in psychoanalytic doctrine.

3. *The Complete Psychological Works of Sigmund Freud*; vol. 10, *Two Case Histories* (London: Hogarth Press, 1968), 3–149.
4. "The Genesis of Agoraphobia," *International Journal of Psychoanalysis* 10 (1929): 51–69.

Contemporary psychiatric theories concerning agora-phobia eschew deep psychoanalytic explanation and center instead on modification of behavior, employing a therapy of desensitization toward the fear-inducing stimulus.[5] This is not to say that behaviorist and cognitive theorists have been unaware of the highly idiosyncratic nature of the syndrome (the quirkiness and intelligence of its sufferers) or of its paradoxes (the combined need for and resentment toward a caretaker, or the simultaneous desire for mobility and need for a safe enclosure).[6]

In recent years, the work of the psychoanalyst Alexandra Symonds has provided an inverse picture from that drawn by contemporary psychiatry, one that has an important, if indirect, bearing on the characters of Elizabeth Abbot and Pamela Emerson in *The Clock Winder.* Symonds counters the conventional depiction of the female agoraphobe as fearing a loss of control (of self, but also environment) this way:

I would like to add another dimension to the understanding of the function that these phobias played in this type of patient. These women were actually afraid to be *in* control. They feared the consequences of taking their life into their own hands, of setting their own direction (as driving a car), of movement on their own, of exploring, of enjoying, of discovering. They feared dealing with the unknown, they feared the ordinary aggression and assertiveness that accompanies growth and involvement. Many years ago, Otto Rank referred to this when he said that more people have a "fear of life" than a "fear of death." The existentialists call it fear of being. Kierkegaard stated in speaking of anxiety "the alarming possibility of being able causes dizziness."[7]

5. For a behaviorist version of the condition that is itself critical of desensitization, see Alan J. Goldstein and Diane L. Chambless, "A Reanalysis of Agoraphobia," *Behavior Therapy* 9 (1978): 47–59.

6. See Aaron T. Beck, Gary Emery, Ruth L. Greenburg, *Anxiety Disorders and Phobias* (New York: Basic Books, 1985), 133–45.

7. "Phobias after Marriage: Women's Declaration of Dependence," in *Psychoanalysis and Women*, ed. Jean Baker Miller (New York: Penguin, 1973), 302.

Symonds comes close to describing the kind of agoraphobia that Tyler's fiction explores, and in the terms she prefers. First, it is located at the self-conscious end of the spectrum, as much a philosophic as a psychiatric condition, a Gordian knot of compulsion and choice. Agoraphobia is a character's imaginative shaping of the world performed in a condition of anxiety. It is an ambivalence toward the question of control so powerful that all aspects of selfhood configurate around it. Second, it is available to novelistic examination, appropriately, on Tyler's "third layer," that of the imaginer, where Freudianism does not flatten its valid imagist content in the name of an inflexible Oedipal explanation, and behaviorism does not ignore it for a therapeutic end.

At this level, Tyler conceptually divides agoraphobia into two opposite tendencies. The first is the fear of victimization. Here the world is perceived as lethal and "home" as a haven of safety. Tyler's key specimens for this variety of agoraphobia are Jeremy Pauling in *Celestial Navigation* and Macon Leary in the first hundred pages of *The Accidental Tourist*. The second tendency correlates with Symonds's description of fear of empowerment, of full engagement in the life one is given, where responsibility leads to the unendurable possibility of guilt. Here one avoids "home" as entrapment, a place where one may do irreparable damage. This second tendency in turn takes two forms. There is flight, characterized by Charlotte Emory in *Earthly Possessions,* and there is dress-up, a metaphor for compulsive fiction-mongering, the demand for "more than one life" of Morgan Gower in *Morgan's Passing.*

Within about a year of writing *The Clock Winder,* Tyler also published two short stories, each dealing with one aspect of this two-sided definition of agoraphobia. The first, "A Misstep of the Mind," is perhaps her darkest, and it is not entirely an accident of publishing that it appeared in *Seventeen* magazine, between ads for Breck Shampoo and a nail-biting preventative called Stop 'n Grow. The story concerns sixteen-year-old Julie Madison, who walks home from school at lunch, interrupts a burglar, and is raped at gunpoint on her living room floor. By invoking the psychologically apt detail, and by avoiding the exploitative, Tyler gives the story an icy verisimilitude. She succeeds in persuading her reader that the menace represented by the young black rapist is a constant aspect of reality. The story attempts to validate the attitude of Macon Leary in *The Accidental Tourist* that agoraphobes enjoy a shortcut to wisdom, that the world is as hostile and dangerous as they suspect. But there is an important difference. *The Accidental Tourist* measures and qualifies Macon's misanthropy, and Macon's wife leaves him because she cannot love a man whose world view is so bleak that he is not shocked by the murder of his son. "A Misstep of the Mind," on the other hand, is a cautionary tale for young readers, which Macon could have written. This story provides a rare instance of narrative intrusion for Tyler. *In propria persona,* she explicitly counsels fear: "She was sensible. If she hadn't been so sensible she might have wondered why the front door had been open on a day when she knew her mother was at the dentist's. She might have listened for a moment before stepping inside; nervousness might have prepared her reflexes for the quick jump backward that might have saved her."[8]

The story sorts out carefully what psychic damage was and was not inflicted on Julie Madison. It ends with a justification of fearfulness that is truly phobic, and with an artistically unjustifiable sense of the complicity of all victims with the world that threatens them—a complicity based solely on the insufficiency of their distrust:

She almost forgot. Her parents forgot, her neighbors forgot, her friends and her boy friend never found out. Yet what she remembered, after everything else had gone, was the packed feeling that the air has when an intruder lies in wait, the capacity for betrayal in a cheerful world where dust floats

8. "A Misstep of the Mind," 118.

54

lazily in sun beams, the knowledge that it is possible to die. She went on expecting, always, to open some door someday and face the sad eyes of a black man, gun raised, head shaking sorrowfully. . . . "Why'd you have to go and open *this* door?" he asked, as he sighed wearily, reproved her with his eyes and aimed his pistol at her head.[9]

Although the story strives to extend a Welty-like sympathy even to the rapist, to give him a life (it is *his* mind that missteps), in the end he is the materialization of the atomistic particles of dread that constitute the atmosphere of an empty house. Here, even "home" betrays, turning into a microcosm for a randomly violent world. The story is powerful; its photographic accuracy supports the apprehension that the inhuman lurks in the ordinary.

The second short story fantasizes a condition of empowerment, a state of mystically validated responsibility that certain of Tyler's characters imagine and evade. "Half-Truths and Semi-Miracles" is the first-person account of Susannah Spright, a small-town Southern woman who possesses the ambiguous gift of healing. She discovers her ability when she is a young girl caring for her Aunt Eunice, who suffers from migraine. Some impulse makes Susannah place her cool hands on Eunice's forehead, and Eunice is immediately cured. At first, Susannah's ability to relieve people's illnesses by laying her hands upon them seems to be a blessing, but soon Susannah finds herself besieged by sufferers and placed outside the pale of ordinary humanity. As she is learning to accept her status as an old maid, a rather undistinguished man at a tent revival confesses his love for her, and they marry. Then, as they are about to accept their childlessness, Susannah becomes pregnant with a son. At the age of six, he is hit by a car; at the hospital, despite her husband's entreaties, Susannah is unable to heal the boy, and he dies. Her husband leaves her, unable to extend any faith toward her after her failure. Subsequently, she begins

9. Ibid., 172.

to envision God as her enemy—the cause of disease rather than the source of her miraculous powers. And she notices that the randomness of her cures persists, unaffected by her decision to curse God rather than pray to him. Lonely and wretched, she visits another healing woman in search of an explanation for the bitter burden she has had to bear:

> Hattie Doone rose up. . . . Then I felt her step around the table and bend to take me in her arms, laying her cheek against mine. She didn't say anything. No words of scripture, no prayers, no laying on of hands, just that long silent hug. . . . I can still remember what I thought she was telling me: it was not God who made you a healer, it was your Aunt Eunice. It was her friend Mrs. Fortney and the man with the lump on his arm and all the others. While they performed their magic, you held tight to their hands. You witnessed their miracles and their semi-miracles and their utter failures. When they said you were responsible, you accepted the burden. What more can anyone do? Now rest awhile. Lean on me. Believe my half-truths, they are all we have.[10]

The story has the clarity of Dostoevskian parable: the obverse of being a victim is being a savior. In these two stories, both positions savor of the uncanny, a magical quality that seems to inform the ordinary but is shown to be nothing more than fear's ability to brighten the edges of perception. In Tyler's version of things, being a savior means allowing other people to entrap you into bearing witness to their pain, allowing them to place the burden of responsibility onto you—and thus to disburden themselves. (In this sense, "Half-Truths and Semi-Miracles" is a preliminary study for the character of Charlotte Emory in *Earthly Possessions*.)

In *The Clock Winder*, a family of inveterate victims finds a reluctant savior, and the result is anxious comedy, reminiscent of the sword fight of Andrew Aguecheek and Feste in Shakespeare's *Twelfth Night*. The novel's principal

10. "Half-Truths and Semi-Miracles," 301–2.

fencers are Mrs. Pamela Emerson, widowed matriarch of the Emerson clan and a committed recluse, and Elizabeth Abbot, a nineteen-year-old North Carolinian in flight from home and responsibility. As the novel opens, Mrs. Emerson fires her black handyman, Richard, for urinating on her rosebushes and hires the drifting Elizabeth in his place. Elizabeth, who is incompetent, finds herself uncannily skilled at solving the maintenance problems of the Emersons' large and crumbling Victorian house in the Roland Park section of Baltimore. But soon she is seduced into more than a casual involvement with the house's inhabitants as well. Timothy Emerson cheats on a medical school exam, gets caught, and locks Elizabeth in the bedroom of his apartment in a crazy attempt to ensnare her in his consequences. Then he involves her in his death when she lunges for the gun with which he threatens to kill himself. Elizabeth flees to her home, allows her parents to push her toward marriage with the insipid Dommie Whitehill, and then abandons him at the altar of her father's Baptist church. Mrs. Emerson suffers a stroke in consequence of a telephone quarrel with her daughter Mary, and the family presses Elizabeth into service as a nurse. Their crazy brother Andrew, an extreme agoraphobe who despises outsiders, blames Elizabeth for Timothy's death and shoots her. The wound is superficial, and Andrew apologizes. There is a three-year hiatus, and then we find Elizabeth, in the last chapter, exactly a decade after Mrs. Emerson hired her as a handyman, living in the house and married to Matthew, the sanest of the Emerson boys. She is the mother of two children, and the entire Emerson family has apparently laid all their burdens, mechanical and emotional, on her shoulders. As the book closes, the youngest son, Peter, and his bride visit and find the house's inhabitants sealed inside against a plague of locusts.

Through this sequence of events, Tyler has distributed her two forms of agoraphobia (locking out assailants, fleeing guilt) to Mrs. Emerson and Elizabeth Abbot respectively. Mrs. Emerson has lost the husband who allowed her to use marriage as an evasion of responsibility, and she approaches—albeit later in life—the kind of crisis that afflicts Symonds's patients when they face the results of choosing wifehood as a method of abdicating autonomy.[11] Symonds wrote: "Marriage for . . . [these women] represents their opportunity to be dependent without self-criticism or self-hate. Marriage then becomes their 'declaration of dependence.' If for any reason this is questioned, or the marriage does not seem to be all they expected, they are in a panic and cling even more."[12] In a passage that reveals the metaphoric significance of clock-winding as control, Tyler provides this self-assessment of Mrs. Emerson:

> She was not a stupid woman, but she was used to being taken care of. She had passed almost without a jolt from the hands of her father to the hands of her husband, an unnoticeable sort of man who since his death had begun to seem much wiser and more mysterious. He knew answers to questions she had not thought of asking, and had kept them to himself. He had wound the clocks absentmindedly, on his way to other places; he had synchronized their striking apparently without effort, without even mentioning it to her—but how? (5–6)

In a sense it is too late for Mrs. Emerson. Her choices were made twenty years earlier, and she operates in the novel as an example of the marital confinement that Elizabeth rejects in her own efforts to evade control. Elizabeth chooses drifting, random mobility, rather than a husband's solicitude as a means of remaining morally unencumbered. Then, at the Emersons, she discovers that she can repair anything, synchronize any number of clocks to strike the hour simultaneously.

11. For a feminist account of marriage as agoraphobic refuge, see Robert Seidenberg and Karen DeCrow, *Women who Marry Houses: Panic and Protest in Agoraphobia* (New York: McGraw Hill, 1983). The authors argue that agoraphobic symptoms are a rhetoric of protest against conventional marriage as confinement of women.

12. "Phobias after Marriage," 299.

Two conditions empower Elizabeth among the Emersons. First is her emotional unconnectedness to the family—the fact that her employment is a sidestep, a self-location outside her destiny as a Baptist minister's dutiful daughter and a future wife to the equally "unnoticeable" Dommie Whitehill back in North Carolina. As with Susannah Spright in "Half-Truths and Semi-Miracles," Elizabeth's powers seem to stem from her having so little life of her own. Elizabeth can welcome her uncanny empowerment only so long as her presence is temporary and her effect is upon the Emersons' material possessions and not the Emersons themselves. (The book insists metaphorically on the difficulty of that distinction: hearts and clocks are much alike.) Elizabeth suffers from a fear of consequentiality. She does not like children because it is easy to have an effect on them. She maintains a principle of arbitrariness in her life by refusing to make decisions. She accepts all invitations, rather than selecting among them, thus evading responsibility for the results. She adopts a belief in reincarnation because it alleviates the pressure of having only one life in which to make choices. She puts her position into words after she returns to North Carolina, tries to marry Dommie, and jilts him at the altar: "Sometimes I worry that everyone but me knows something I don't know: they set out their lives without *wondering,* as if they had a few extras stashed away somewhere. Well, I've tried to believe it, but I can't. Things are so permanent. There's damage you can't repair" (202).

Mrs. Emerson, like Symonds's patients, fled to marriage as a means of escaping just this sense of consequentiality. Elizabeth is quirkier and more perceptive. She locates herself in the accidental, getting rides and jobs from laundromat bulletin boards, in an anxious parody of Oedipus's attempts at evading his own fate. Thus, she is a dialectically inverted agoraphobe, safe in a house only if it is not her own but safer yet in that icon of mobility, the automobile:

"Elizabeth is so devoted to bulletin boards," Mrs. Emerson said. "I never even knew they existed. She finds them everywhere—laundromats, thrift shops, university buildings. She always knows who is driving where and who has lost what and who is selling their old diamonds off."

"In this weather a train would be safer," Matthew said.

"I prefer cars," said Elizabeth. "They give you the feeling you can get off wherever you like."

"But why would you want to get off?" Timothy asked.

"Oh, I wouldn't. I just like to know I can." (49)

The second condition that empowers Elizabeth is her availability as witness. She is not busy; she can watch. Her presence alleviates the stifling atmosphere of this self-involved family. Elizabeth perceives the way the world's victims exploit their saviors; without acknowledging her complicity, she benefits from the peculiar meshing of her gears with those of the Emersons. Nevertheless, she resents their use of her:

"You must think our family is pretty crazy," Margaret said after a while.

"More or less."

It wasn't the answer she had expected. "They aren't *really*," she said, too loudly. Then she sighed and said, "Oh well, I guess they *could* wear on your nerves quite a bit."

Elizabeth stayed quiet.

"Dragging you into all our troubles that way. It must—"

"Ha," said Elizabeth.

"What?"

"They didn't drag me *in*, they wanted me for an audience." She clipped off the ends of her words, as if she were angry. "I finally saw that," she said. "I was hired to watch. I couldn't have helped if I tried. I wasn't supposed to." (193)

At a key point in the novel, moments before Timothy Emerson's death, Elizabeth tests the fantasy of magical empowerment. Timothy has been caught cheating on his medical school exam and has attempted to place the disaster on Elizabeth's shoulders. When she will not go away with him for the weekend or respond seriously to his sense of panic, he locks her in his bedroom, where she lights a match and holds it:

> The matches she struck one by one on the windowsill and then held in her fingers, testing to see if telepathy could make a flame go out before it burned her. It couldn't. She was relieved to see the flickering knot of blue proceed steadily downward, unaffected by anything so insubstantial as her thought waves, which flickered also, veering from the match in her hand to the silent figure behind the door. (89)

The Clock Winder is a meditation on the power that inheres in the role of witness. Its narrative technique attains a density of texture that subsequent novels have simplified without a loss in complexity of vision. Of all Tyler's works, *The Clock Winder* and *Searching for Caleb* have the most brushstrokes. But that density serves Tyler's developing idea of selfhood as a pattern in time. Here, point of view is subject as well as technique, and it is defined as one narrative consciousness, in flight from a predicament, bearing witness to the predicaments of others. Evasion and perception are linked, and the mind in flight is the one that sees most in a situation parallel to its own.

Chapter 9, set in 1963, serves as a convenient model for the novel's perceptual principle. When Margaret Emerson was young, she ran off with the boy who delivered the Emersons' groceries. After five weeks of marriage, she and Jimmy Joe opened their apartment door and allowed Mrs. Emerson to step in, pack Margaret's possessions, and take her home. Later, Margaret married sensibly, but she begins to wake up at night crying uncontrollably with nostalgia and guilt for her first love. Haunted by her past and in flight from the solicitude of her present husband, she drives to North Carolina to attend (and witness) Elizabeth's wedding to Dommie Whitehill, the boy her parents want her to marry, whose personality is a dead match for Jimmy Joe's.

Thus it comes about that we watch over Margaret's

shoulder as Elizabeth strands Dommie at the altar. Elizabeth's father sees that something is wrong, and he rushes the ceremony. When he arrives at the vows, Elizabeth blurts out, "I don't. I'm sorry. I just don't." She then marches out of the church, hides in Margaret's car, and allows Margaret to drive her to freedom. The narrative effects of this doubling of patterned response give the book its peculiar richness. Margaret applauds Elizabeth's rebellion as a form of courage—it was precisely the defiance of parental control that she failed to summon in her own past. The patterns are reversed as in a mirror: Elizabeth's forced marriage to, and Margaret's forced separation from, a gentle, ineffectual boy. Margaret understandably praises Elizabeth for her bravery, but Elizabeth contradicts her, arguing that real courage lies not in escape but in the kind of plodding commitment that she fears far more than embarrassment:

> "*Flashes* of courage are easy," said Elizabeth, with her mind on something else. Then suddenly she spun around and said, "What's the matter with you? What are you admiring so much? If I was so brave, how'd I get into that wedding in the *first* place? Oh, think about Dommie, he's always so sweet and patient." (202)

What is delicious here—and what affirms the mystery of character—is that apparently Margaret does think about Dommie, and in turn about her own past, and finds herself cured of her nostalgia for Jimmy Joe. There is no moral position that emerges from this intricate narration. The fiction gives us superimposed and reversed patterns of love, parental intrusion, failure of courage, guilt, and escape. It indicates that these are important; they happen to people. What Tyler—who is like Elizabeth in her reticence—refuses to do is give advice, advocate. Consistently in this book, when actions occur, the narrative makes it clear that exactly the opposite could have happened. Elizabeth abandoned Dommie; she almost married him. Margaret let her mother take her from Jimmy

Joe; years later she was paralyzed with regret. Timothy fired the gun and died; he might as easily have laughed at the scene's absurdity. Andrew shot Elizabeth; then he comforted her.

As Margaret bears witness to Elizabeth in this chapter, so Elizabeth bears witness to the Emersons in the novel's overarching structure, which moves from a first section covering Elizabeth's first sojourn in Baltimore, to a middle section detailing her attempt to return to her past in North Carolina, to a conclusion in Baltimore again. Elizabeth's past has shaped the pattern of her responses, defined her predicament, in ways that are both paralleled and opposed (that is, musically counterpointed) in the Emerson household. Yet Tyler withholds the story of Elizabeth's past until the middle section, so that we see the *pattern* of her avoidance of responsibility before we see its origins.

Examples of counterpoint are numerous and subtle. The Emerson parents are variants of Elizabeth's. Elizabeth's father and mother are as inexhaustible in their cataloging of her derelictions of duty as Mrs. Emerson is with her children. In one telling juxtaposition, Elizabeth overhears Mrs. Emerson reciting litanies of complaint against her offspring into her dictaphone. Elizabeth goes to her room and rereads a letter from her mother that is indistinguishable from Mrs. Emerson's monologue. Or consider Elizabeth's incompetence at home. Revealed first as a tendency toward self-distrust, we witness it as event when Elizabeth returns to North Carolina, watches television, sleeps until 11:00 A.M., and walks the dog for employment. This is a mirror image of the chronic uselessness of the male Emerson children. One has only to recall the scene of the Emersons' collectively acute anxiety when Matthew tries to light a fire in the family hearth. And Matthew is the only one who can contribute to the house's maintenance.

With the exception of Timothy's death, it is primarily generational conflict that provides forward impetus to *The Clock Winder* and sets up its opportunities for counter-

63

point. In a wonderfully comic sequence, Mrs. Emerson phones her daughter Mary to wheedle an invitation to come and babysit while Mary and her husband are on vacation. Mrs. Emerson is a master at engineering her own emotional defeats, and Mary has a daughter's perverse eagerness to conspire with her in that project. When Mary recites a list of Mrs. Emerson's offenses on her last visit, Mrs. Emerson collapses from a stroke. The scene is in every way gentler than the similar one in Flannery O'Connor's "Everything That Rises Must Converge," in which Julian tells off his mother for her absurd racial pride and she collapses on the sidewalk. In reusing this fantasy of the guilty child, Tyler domesticates O'Connor; where Julian's mother turns into a grotesque heap, seen from above, Mrs. Emerson remains the narrative center of her own collapse. Having fallen under the dining room table, she is outraged at finding the chewing gum that one of her children had stuck under the leaf.

Mrs. Emerson's stroke sets a number of consequences in motion. First, it leaves her unable to finish a sentence, thus terminating her guilt-inflicting monologue. On the other hand, it forces her children (and later Elizabeth) to come home and finish sentences for her, ironically the thing she wanted all along. Also, she pronounces Elizabeth's name "Gillespie"—a transformation that the entire family adopts, signaling Elizabeth's assumption of a new identity that is not entirely her own but that can be entered into like fiction. "The name 'Gillespie' rang in her ears—the new person Mrs. Emerson was changing her into, someone effective and managerial who was summoned by her last name, like a WAC" (244–45). Her final renaming occurs with marriage to Andrew, when "Elizabeth Abbott" is reborn as "Gillespie Emerson," a culmination of the efforts she has shown throughout the book to evade specificity, including that of gender. It is a sane avoidance of the consequences of Mrs. Emerson's femininity.

Actually, the compromise signaled by Elizabeth's name— she will become a wife and mother but remain a handy-

man—also seems to necessitate the maiming of Mrs. Emerson, who, like Mr. Rochester in *Jane Eyre,* must be reduced in capacity before any emotional contact is possible. The stroke extinguishes the voice that represented a perversion of power to control through weakness and dependency—the cause and witness of the family's troubles. Thus the plot of *The Clock Winder* is a cautiously negotiated contract of obligation. An open-eyed set of compromises transforms an anxious and evasive girl into an adult who at least manages to be overburdened on her own terms, and who will be neither the practitioner nor the victim of emotional blackmail.

In an interview with Clifford Ridley, Tyler spoke of the entrapment of Elizabeth in a manner that underscores the book's artistic agenda as an examination of character as emotional pattern, rather than a moral treatise for or against caretaking: "In many ways *The Clock Winder* condemns what it praises and vice-versa; I think Elizabeth does herself irreparable damage in not going farther than she does, but on the other hand what she does is the happiest and best thing for her. I think of it as a sad ending, and I've been surprised that not everybody does."[13] Tyler seems to discount the emotional price Elizabeth paid for the enforced inconsequentiality of her youth. There is comedy—even charm—in her efforts at irrelevance. But the novel's logic implies that Elizabeth's eventual entrapment is in fact happier than the strenuously maintained insouciance that kept her on the margins of all intercourse.

The final pages of *The Clock Winder* describe a visit home by Peter, the youngest of the Emersons and the one who grew up at a distance from the turmoil. Peter's predicament rests in his bringing home a countrified bride from Georgia whom he has forgotten to tell the family about. As he becomes a final witness of the state of affairs of the Emerson household, it is August 1970, exactly ten years since Richard urinated on the rosebushes and Mrs. Emer-

13. Clifford Ridley, "Anne Tyler: A Sense of Reticence Balanced by 'Oh, Well, Why Not?'"

son hired Elizabeth to take his place. Peter finds the family in altered circumstances. "Gillespie's" older child, George, is playing with a live locust on the porch. In the kitchen, she carries an infant on her hip. The rest of the family is sealed inside the house, afraid to leave it until the cessation of the seventeen-year-locust plague. The circumstance provides a metaphor—the family is no less agoraphobic or involuted for Elizabeth's presence. In fact, if anything, her caretaking has allowed them to indulge their incompetence even further. Perhaps, like Shakespeare, Tyler is reserving her old age for the creation of transformative happy endings.

IV CELESTIAL NAVIGATION

DESPITE her reclusiveness, Anne Tyler over the past decade and a half has granted a handful of interviews, written a few autobiographical accounts of her composing habits, and taken part in a symposium at Duke University, where she had been a student in Reynolds Price's writing class.[1] In all these places, Tyler speaks of but one aspect of her personal life—her writing routine. She says she spends about six hours a day alone in a white room. She acknowledges a need to avoid experience when she is writing (she even avoids serious reading during the initial drafting stages of a novel). She speaks gratefully of the support of her husband, Tagi Modaressi, an Iranian-born psychiatrist and himself a novelist by avocation. She admits—in a tone of bemusement—that her books possess a will of their own: each demands that it be finished, no matter how bad it may seem, before the next one can begin. She speaks—again bemusedly—of the longing that comes over her to live in a boathouse and write for twenty-three hours a day.[2]

The tone of Tyler's autobiographical accounts is always bemusement. For her, such revelations are trivial, feeding a misguided popular hunger for news about the personal life of the artist, who works solely in order to imagine lives *other* than her own. Tyler remains subtly evasive in all her nonfictional self-representations. Besides the tone, that evasiveness lies in details. The cir-

1. See, for instance, "Because I Want More than One Life"; "Olives Out of a Bottle" [Symposium at Duke University]; Clifford Ridley, "Anne Tyler: A Sense of Reticence Balanced by 'Oh, Well, Why Not?'"; "Still Just Writing," in *The Writer and Her Work: Contemporary Women Writers Reflect on Their Art and Situation,* ed. Janet Sternberg; and "A Visit with Eudora Welty." This last interview is as much about Tyler's reclusiveness as about Welty's.

2. Compare "The Bride in the Boatyard." The story locates such absolute creative isolation in the realm of psychosis.

cumstances she proffers about her life seem rehearsed, a repertoire of those few things she has chosen to say on such occasions.

As a fictional subject, however, artistic withdrawal is a fascinating and serious matter to Tyler. It constitutes a mode of perception. Therefore, the term *autobiographical* in the discussion that follows does not mean "personally revealing." Instead, it represents an inference that Tyler has drawn upon observations of the emotional dynamics of her own imagination in order to isolate for study an agoraphobic element in art. Jeremy Pauling is an autobiographical creation of Tyler's in the sense that Henry J. Waugh is an autobiographical creation of Robert Coover's. Coover is not an alcoholic accountant, and Tyler does not collapse in front of grocery stores. But, as the *Universal Baseball Association* is a meditation on the paradoxes of debasement inherent in creative power, so *Celestial Navigation* is a meditation on the connection between disorientation and insight.

Tyler's public pronouncements are apparently coy but actually cagey. Her strategy of self-bemusement permits her to tell the truth in the wrong register—a deception worthy of Poe's Dupin. I will quote her closing comments from a rather bland panel discussion held at Duke University in 1975 on the lives of young novelists. Throughout the text, the editors indicate the frequent moments when Tyler's observations moved the audience to laughter, charmed by her protestations that she never takes more than two steps toward madness. In context, these words conclude a jovial conversation. But take them out of context, ignore the charm, and their tone darkens considerably:

Yes. Anything I've ever written I've wanted to know how much dependency is allowed between people, how much right people have to want to change other people. All that business. And I resent the fact that blurbs on my books always say I'm concerned with lack of communication because I don't think communication is really all that hot between people. I don't think it's necessary or desirable in lots of cases.[3]

The comment sweetly damns the occasion. It has the kind of edge found in the best moments of Tyler's fiction, when bemusement at the oddity of character gives way and the reader confronts something important—that it is sentimental and even dangerous to overvalue "communication." At any given time, behind *some* door, a man with a gun is waiting.

In a letter to Stella Nesanovich, Tyler marked the beginning point in the evolution of her artist-protagonist as a moment in the Duke University Library, where she worked as a bibliographer: "I was once supposed to supervise the library training of a very pale, pudgy, frightened man who had just been released from a mental hospital, and I was disturbed because no matter how gently I spoke to him, he was overwhelmed, and would back off, stammering. He only lasted a day and then vanished forever, but five years of thinking about him produced Jeremy."[4]

Over the next decade and a half, Tyler transmuted this frightened man into a kaleidoscopic series of variations on the theme of reticence as a cognitive style. As she says, he first appears as the agoraphobic sculptor/junk constructionist Jeremy Pauling. Jeremy is actually Tyler's most radical variant psychologically, and *Celestial Navigation* is her most theoretical book, in essence a poetics of agoraphobia. In Jeremy, Tyler recasts the novelist's inventive processes in the guise of a consciousness so fragmentary and fleeting that it approaches autism. The figure re-emerges as Ezra Tull, the unassuming genius of nurture and noninvasion in *Dinner at the Homesick Restaurant,* and has reappeared most recently as Macon Leary, author of the "Accidental Tourist" series of travel books for people

3. "Olives Out of a Bottle," 81.
4. Stella Nesanovich, "The Individual in the Family: A Critical Introduction to the Novels of Anne Tyler," 123.

who cannot leave home. Tyler speaks, in "Because I Want More than One Life," of "my favorite hero, a shy, pudgy man, waiting hopefully by the railroad tracks with his clumsy little suitcase." The Tyler artist is also blond, pale, balding, wide-hipped, rather sexless, compassionately alert, and deeply, comically unaggressive. While the circumstances of his biography vary from one novel to the next, his life is a tenacious philosophical inquiry into a single question, most succinctly stated by Ezra Tull (and most swiftly ignored by his mother Pearl):

> "I'm worried I don't know how to get in touch with people," Ezra said.
> "Hmm?"
> "I'm worried if I come too close, they'll say I'm overstepping. They'll say I'm pushy, or . . . emotional, you know. But if I back off, they might think I don't care. I really, honestly believe I missed some rule that everyone else takes for granted; I must have been absent from school that day. There's this narrow little dividing line I somehow never located."
> "Nonsense; I don't know what you're talking about," said his mother, and then she held up an egg.[5]

Of the three fictional versions of herself, Tyler has given Jeremy Pauling the closest scrutiny as a working artist, and his work most directly reflects her own. Macon Leary's books about travel are fraught with the paradoxes of the writer who resists experience, but their presence in *The Accidental Tourist* is largely objectified—a revision to finish, a deadline to be met. In *Dinner at the Homesick Restaurant*, Ezra's cooking is a metaphorical step or two away from novel-writing, although his "consoling pot roasts" and gizzard soup "made with love" are surely parables about the novelist's proper labor, distance, and sympathy. On the contrary, Jeremy's "pieces" are tightly analogous to Tyler's novels, providing her with an opportunity for critical discourse. *Celestial Navigation* is Tyler's vigorous

5. *Dinner at the Homesick Restaurant* (New York: Berkeley Books, 1983), 127.

search for compulsive roots beneath a "realist" imagination, one that is endlessly engaged in constructing inventories of the mundane. Tyler has written that she sometimes envies Gabriel García Márquez, who can imagine José Arcadio Buendía's blood traveling through the house, "hugging the walls so as not to stain the carpets," while she worries "who takes cream and who doesn't."[6] What it means so to worry, what such worrying costs a life, is the darker subject of *Celestial Navigation*.

Tyler provides an icon of artistic compulsion in Jeremy's most celebrated sculpture. Unwillingly, Jeremy allows himself to be taken to a one-man show of his work at a local gallery owned by his wealthy, competent agent, Brian O'Donnell. There, he sees his own piece:

> In the foyer, lit by a yellow light, was a piece that Jeremy remembered from three or four years ago: an old man going through a wire trashbasket. The man himself was made of dull brown wrapping paper, crushed and reflattened. The basket was a network of all the glittery things he had been able to lay his hands on—small skewers for trussing poultry, a knitting needle, a child's gilt barrette, a pair of Abbie's school scissors with "Lefty" on the blade. Within the basket was a cluster of bright colors formed from postage stamps and cigarette packs and an old bandanna handkerchief that Mr. Somerset had left lying on the couch one day. "Haven't they done it nicely?" Mary asked him. "I told Brian, it's the perfect keynote for the show. I'm glad they set it up at the beginning this way."
>
> "Yes, yes," said Jeremy. But he was uncomfortable.[7]

The distinct layering of the reader's attention here—the little wire man rummaging through junk, Jeremy's assemblage of him, Tyler's minutely detailed rendering of both of them as an ironic version of her own realism—

6. "Writers' Writers," *New York Times Book Review,* 4 December 1977, 70.

7. *Celestial Navigation* (New York: Berkeley Books, 1984), 146. Hereafter cited parenthetically in the text by page number.

marks this novel as metafictional. Both the novelist and her character—like the captain who sails by the stars—rely on an illusory ordering of external objects to orient them in the world, to fend off terror. "Celestial Navigation" is a metaphor for a style of consciousness that expresses itself—and finds a degree of cosmic safety—in the act of making an inventory.

The novel documents Jeremy's agoraphobia. He is unable to leave the block he lives on. He retreats to the third-floor studio of his family home (which he turned into a boardinghouse in order to have a source of income that would not require him to step outside). He suffers panic reactions and relies on "safe" people like his mother and Mary Tell. Tyler meticulously stitches these agoraphobic traits with his fragmented, radically sequential, memory-impaired consciousness. A number of the determinants of Jeremy's mind reflect things Tyler has said about herself and not only demonstrate Jeremy's role as a "portrait of the artist" but also constitute a fascinating inquiry into the role phobic consciousness plays in the act of representation, the way panic can elicit the moment of epiphany, when there is fuzzy light at the edges of the object and the world reassembles itself on an altered moral grid.

Nesanovich has recorded Jeremy's similarities to his creator, their need to work on one project at a time (the phrase "olives out of a bottle" is used to describe Jeremy's work on page 205 of *Celestial Navigation*), their love of solitude and longing for the whitewashed cubicle, and their forgetfulness. For both Tyler and Jeremy, ideas have a reified quality: they pass through the brain like railroad cars whose serial numbers must be swiftly recorded or lost forever. And their vision is atomistic. Nesanovich quotes from a letter to her in which Tyler acknowledged that she "sneakily donated little pieces of herself" to Jeremy, especially her "habit of seeing the slits in the screws of the electrical outlet but not the room as a whole."[8]

8. "The Individual in the Family," 124.

The world of *Celestial Navigation* rests on the same perceptual scale:

> When Jeremy was seven he made a drawing of his mother's parlor. Long slashes for walls and ceiling, curves for furniture, a single scribbled rose denoting the wallpaper pattern. And then, on the baseboard, a tiny electrical socket, its right angles crisp and precise, its screws neatly bisected by microscopic slits. It was his sister Laura's favorite picture. She kept it for years, and laughed everytime she looked at it, but he had never meant it to be a joke. That was the way his vision functioned: only in detail. Piece by piece. He had tried looking at the whole of things but it never worked out. He tried now, widening his eyes to take in the chilly white air below the skylight and the bare yellow plaster and splintery floors. The angles of the walls raced toward each other and collided. Gigantic hollow space loomed over him, echoing. The brightness made his lids ache. (38–39)

There is a mechanistic quality to the drawing—its draftsmanlike precision dedicated to one object, and that object arbitrarily hit on, tenaciously clung to, isolated from the dizzying chaos around it. Such a drawing implies a sense of reality as an endless series of discrete things. Furthermore, one sees a deep passivity in the phobic artist's method. Ideas happen to him. Agoraphobia is characterized by efforts to avoid a panic reaction—a specific kind of sensory overload. As Tyler defines it through Jeremy, it occurs when one feels one cannot process the world swiftly enough, operating one object at a time. The consequence is disorientation in the presence of a vertiginous receding space, a world that will not be controlled through inventory. Thus, peace for Jeremy lies in working in a confined space, gluing fragments of perception together in an order he himself imposes. This is tantamount to magical thinking in that the correspondences that unify the work are paralogical, like puns. (Recall the anecdote about James Joyce, who put a pho-

tograph of the city of Cork, Ireland, in a cork frame.[9]
Finnegans Wake is the same act expanded to the proportions of a pseudo-cosmos.) The happy consequence of such construction is the comfort an alternative, illusory universe provides. Of the four characters who narrate this book, the one who understands Jeremy's work is the lady who leaves him alone, Miss Vinton. She describes one of Jeremy's constructions:

> It's strange how over the years Jeremy's pieces have grown up. I mean physically, literally. They have doubled in size, and they are so deeply textured that they are almost sculptures. Ordinary objects are crowded into them—Dixie cups and bus tickets and his children's plaid shoelaces, still recognizable— and his subjects are ordinary too, the smallest and most unnoticed scenes on earth. I found a man with a rake, a woman ironing a shirt, a child strapping on a roller skate. Their features were gone and they were bare of detail; they were layered over with the Dixie cups and the bus tickets. They made me sad.
>
> . . . This man with the rake, slightly stooped and motionless, reminded me that life is nothing *but* motion and passes too swiftly for us to observe with the naked eye. At least for me to observe. Jeremy has no trouble whatsoever. He sees from a distance at all times, without trying, even trying not to. It is his condition. He *lives* at a distance. He makes pictures the way other men make maps—setting down the few fixed points that he knows, hoping that they will guide him as he goes floating through this unfamiliar planet. He keeps his eyes on the horizon while his hands work blind. (129)

Surely this fictional self-portrait counteracts the blandness of Tyler's autobiographical testimony and admits to a degree of compulsion behind her cataloging of the physical items of middle-class American culture. Jeremy Pauling is Tyler's self-caricature as a primitive artist. He cannot describe what he does, and he cannot control the life

9. Richard Ellmann, *James Joyce* (New York: Oxford University Press, 1959, 1982), 551.

he leads when he is not working. He represents an absolute—that boathouse to which Tyler imagines herself retreating to work twenty-three hours a day. Thus the tale of Jeremy's union with and breaking from Mary Tell is an act of autobiographical speculation. Is an artist happier without self-consciousness? What lies on the other side of a total surrender to compulsion?

The evolution of Jeremy's art provides the answer— *misery with compensations.* Tyler fastidiously describes the growth of Jeremy's work over his years since art school, years of increasing reclusiveness and growing inability to negotiate the practical world.[10] As his "pieces" shift from collage and mosaic toward sculpture and ultimately toward shadow boxes, their subject is increasingly that of solitude; what they contain, more and more, is emptiness. And emptiness is the precise content of the last work of Jeremy's that we see in the novel. Here is Olivia's description of the box Jeremy made as an homage to Mary:

Imagine a wooden soft drink crate, only bigger, standing on end. A set of compartments, and in each compartment a different collection of objects. Like an advertisement showing a cross-section of a busy household. . . . Only in Jeremy's piece there were no people. Only the *feeling* of people—of full lives suddenly interrupted, belongings still bearing the imprint of their vanished owners. Dark squares upstairs full of toys, paper scraps, a plastic doll bed lying on its side as if some burst of exuberance had flung it there and then passed on, leaving such a vacancy it could make you cry. (221)

10. Jeremy and his work bear a coincidental resemblance to the New York boxmaker and junk sculptor Joseph Cornell (1903–1972). One of Cornell's collages, *No. 244 Untitled (Ship with Nude),* shows a woman's upper torso superimposed upon the bow of a ship, her right arm extending on the bowsprit, and a star map superimposed on her abdomen, connecting the idea of celestial navigation with the nurturing female figure. Cornell's sister liked to tell a story of Cornell's adolescence. One night she had found him in his room, trembling; he had had to drop his astronomy course because the talk of infinity gave him anxiety attacks.

Jeremy's box achieves an eloquence on the subject of absence, and surely eloquence compensates. The sculpture adumbrates a central idea in Tyler's subsequent books, that of "homesickness." It begins the complex unpacking of the familiar term that continues in *Dinner at the Homesick Restaurant* and *The Accidental Tourist*, where the word comes to mean not only sickness for home (longing, nostalgia) but also sickness of it (the need to escape from the invasiveness of family) and sickness from it (the psychic wounds that human beings inevitably carry as a result of having had to grow up as children in families). Tyler conceptualizes her fictions spatially, designing them to suggest ideal emotional distances between people. Paradoxically, it is the artist as inspired witness who requires the greatest distance of all.

On her way to inventing her supreme depictions of this utopian emotional state—Macon's winged armchair, Ezra's restaurant that is not a home but is as a home might be—Tyler experimented with a Jamesian version in *Celestial Navigation*, the boardinghouse of fiction. Jeremy's last sculpture is a miniature of his boardinghouse and a paradigm of the novel that contains them both, which is narrated by people who are characters in the fiction and inhabitants of the house. Since Jeremy is a version of his creator, all these narrators use the space their artist *cum* host provides to comment upon his/her remoteness from them.

As a house of fiction, the book's architecture is richly symmetrical. In ten chapters, it covers roughly a decade of events. The first half, occurring in the early 1960s, relates the courtship and union of Jeremy Pauling and Mary Tell. The second half, occurring in the early 1970s, records their dissolution. Like bookends, two intrusive character-narrators, Jeremy's sister Amanda and the "hippie girl" Olivia, respectively, delineate the opening and closing events. Two more reticent characters, Miss Vinton and Mary Tell, have two narrative sections each— Mary once in each half; Miss Vinton in an interlude (set in 1968) and an epilogue. Finally, four sections adapt the

76

conventional limited-omniscient voice to Jeremy's fragmentary style of consciousness to provide—ventriloquially—his own view of things. A study of the book's five different narrative voices reveals the importance of reticence and retreat: Tyler allows Miss Vinton, who is painfully reticent, the deepest understanding of Jeremy; Amanda, who is inquisitorial, has no understanding at all.

For Tyler, a novel and a living arrangement share two desirable aspects: they should not crowd anyone (character, reader, or author; owner or tenant), and they should change (intrusion is only slightly worse than tedium). Thus Macon Leary's travelers' series must constantly be updated ("Things are changing every minute, Macon. Change! It's what keeps us in the black," his publisher tells him).[11] Ezra's menus are posted daily on a blackboard, and Jeremy's boardinghouse has a rotating medical student in the front bedroom, a young man who will always have habits that annoy the older boarders, habits that will change with each new student, every two years. Likewise, Tyler's fictions will persist in their study of the ideal distances between people, but their characters will change. She will always look forward to saying goodbye to them, ushering them cordially out of her white study, before they become tedious.[12]

Miss Vinton, holder of the spinster position in Jeremy's house, states Tyler's position almost exactly, so I will begin this inventory of the novel's narrators with her:

If you want my opinion, our whole society would be better off living in boarding houses. I mean even families, even married couples. Everyone should have his single room with a door that locks, and then a larger room downstairs where people can mingle or not as they please. For I do like *some* people. I'm no hermit. I like to watch Jeremy's and Mary's children growing up, and the medical students that turn into

11. *The Accidental Tourist* (New York: Alfred A. Knopf, 1988), 90.

12. But Doris Betts has imagined all Tyler's characters from the separate novels coexisting as members of some huge metafictional clan. See "The Fiction of Anne Tyler," 34–35.

doctors, and Mr. Somerset shuffling through his pension. For such a good life, isn't it fair that I should have to pay some price? The price is silence. (125–26)

Miss Vinton is a persona of the novelist; she too loves change (a proximity to people that lets her meditate on their patterned instability), and she is deeply reticent. Yet it is Miss Vinton who intuits Mary's plight as Jeremy withdraws from their union. At the novel's end, she, rather than the vital Mary or the clairvoyant Olivia, remains as Jeremy's proper companion. Miss Vinton ends the novel with a vignette of herself and Jeremy, navigating home from a journey to the supermarket. With the gift of negative capability, she sees herself and Jeremy through the eyes of a boy on a doorstep:

We trundle down the sidewalk like two clay ducks, and the boy on the stoop yawns and reaches for a beer. If he looks at us at all he sees only an elderly couple, together no doubt for centuries, arriving at the end of their dusty and unremarkable lives. The woman's cardigan is drab and frayed. The man wears crocheted bedroom slippers. He seems peaceful but distant, detached from his surroundings. The boy starts whistling a lighthearted tune, and he goes on whistling long after the elderly couple has turned in at the house near the corner and locked the door and drawn the window shades. (249)

It is a quietly self-reflexive ending, with the novel and the boardinghouse closing up simultaneously, in a muted echo of the self-referential endings of Poe's "Fall of the House of Usher" or García Márquez's *One Hundred Years of Solitude*.

Other narrators are not reticent at all. The book opens in the voice of Jeremy's unhappy spinster sister, Amanda, who has known no real love. She is a stereotype of the old maid schoolteacher, and she knows it: "There are a thousand jokes about the likes of me. None of them are funny" (34). Her narrative, in its rancor toward Jeremy, is spicily reminiscent of Jason Compson's depictions of Benjy in his section of *The Sound and the Fury.* When their mother has had a heart attack on the stairs, climbing to see Jeremy's new work, Amanda wonders if she did not die "for a little paper quilt put together by a middle-aged man" (20). Amanda wants more emotional involvement from her family than Jeremy or their mother provides, and her revenge is to see Jeremy as a freak, whose crazy reclusiveness is nothing more than a failure of courage. She forces him to walk to the funeral parlor where their mother is laid out, and he collapses in panic on the sidewalk. When their sister Laura becomes angry and leads Jeremy home, Amanda says: "I walked six paces behind, all alone. Well, there are worse things than walking alone. Look at Jeremy, propped up on both sides, beloved son of Wilma Pauling. If that is what love does to you, isn't it possible that I am the most fortunate of us all?" (34).

Amanda (whose name, of course, means "worthy of love") records several of the darker truths about the agoraphobic artist: regressiveness, self-absorption, emotional unreliability. Yet Amanda bears a family resemblance to Jeremy, and to Tyler as well. Her narrative section is an inventory, a loveless one that nevertheless resembles Jeremy's sculpture of the boardinghouse in that it too is a catalog of absences. For instance, upon arriving at the house, Amanda and Laura find it locked; thinking Jeremy is at the funeral parlor, they leave their suitcases in the front vestibule. When they return, they discover that Jeremy was at home all the time, and the suitcases have been stolen. Amanda records the loss:

> Here are the other belongings I had in that suitcase: my brown wool suit that was appropriate for any occasion, my blouse with the Irish lace at the collar, the lingerie set Laura gave me for my birthday. Also my travel alarm, the folding one that Mrs. Evans sent the summer I accompanied her twins on a tour of Yosemite. *That* was gone now. And my flowered duster that packed so well, and my warmest nightgown and the fleece-lined slippers that always felt so good when I came home tired from a long day at school. You couldn't replace things like that. (35)

Although her life has led her to advocate all the joyless forms of responsibility, and her suitcase reveals a sensibility of severe limitation, Amanda does have an artistic side. Ruefully, she understands that objects demand that we see them accurately because they are going to disappear. She deliciously imagines the fate of her stolen lisle stockings, capturing a moment as vivid and whimsical as anything in Jeremy's work, a moment that reveals by its inclusion that Tyler had no simplistic purposes for her character:

> And here I had put that brand-new pair in my suitcase! They hadn't even been taken out of the cellophane yet! Quality hose, with fine seams. (We were raised to believe that no true lady wears seamless stockings, although I must say that nowadays people don't appear to agree.) Now some burglar's wife was probably trying my nylons on. I pictured her lolling on a brass bed in a red lace slip, one leg in the air, smoothing a stocking up her thigh while the burglar sat in an armchair smoking a fat cigar and watching. "Who did these belong to once?" "Oh, some old biddy." (35)

Of all the versions of the artist that the narrators of *Celestial Navigation* represent, none outstrips Amanda for wit or self-awareness. The center of her resentment is the house itself. She grew up in it; Jeremy has inherited it. And he has turned it into a boardinghouse, the symbol of change and distance, the two things she despises.

The homeless hippie girl Olivia experiences a similar rejection by Jeremy and his house. Her narrative section begins on the day Mary packs up the children and leaves Jeremy. Olivia's style is a farrago of popular cultural clichés from television, movies, and vegetarian cookbooks, combined with a clairvoyance that, like Jeremy's genius, seems to be a compensation for other inadequacies. Olivia turns to Jeremy upon Mary's departure in order to be "defined" by him. Resenting Mary's security of role, and feeling without an identity herself, Olivia invades Jeremy's consciousness along with his studio, until they achieve a shared psyche. Offended by the polite distance of Miss Vinton, Olivia declares, "Aloofness is the easy way, I believe in plunging right ahead" (203). Soon, Olivia stares into the same empty spaces that occupy Jeremy's vision and knows what Jeremy is dreaming. They sink together into a profound listlessness that cancels any gains Olivia has made in escaping from her isolation, since there is nothing but television to occupy their clairvoyance. The final irony is devastating. Olivia insists that Jeremy accompany her upstairs to the studio, where they have not been in weeks; once there, however, she grasps the meaning of Jeremy's sculpture—it is a paean to Mary. She packs her suitcase and leaves; but while hitchhiking in the street she discovers that she has become infected, not with Jeremy's talent, but with his agoraphobia. She watches a Cadillac roll by and thinks: "Please, lady! I'm only eighteen and a girl to boot, and it seems much brighter and colder out here than I had expected. I didn't know the sky would be so wide today" (222).

In a sense, Olivia (perhaps the name is a sly reference to the novelist herself, who gets her work like "olives from a bottle") mirrors Jeremy more exactly than his other narrators; certainly she achieves an intimacy with him that crosses the bounds of realism. Jeremy acknowledges that she has remained with him when everyone else in his life has died or left, but he feels that she is not "outside" him and therefore is not another person. She is the paradigm of the novelist's activity—an observer without an identity, a character narrator who approaches the anonymity of the limited-omniscient voice that narrates Jeremy's own sections.

Celestial Navigation unites Jeremy and Mary to delineate the paradox of agoraphobic art—the longing to live more than one life coupled with the need to retreat into a privacy so complete that it is no life at all. Thus Mary Tell is—in her omnicompetence and unfrightened appetite for experience—the narrator who balances and opposes Jeremy's highly filtered vision of the world. In a sense, Jeremy and Mary constitute between them the rhythm of

Tyler's working day, divided into six hours of absolute retreat and eighteen of busy, upper-middle-class motherhood.[13] Just as Jeremy and Mary end up separated, Tyler has indicated that the conscious shift from one part of her day to another is a painful changing of worlds:

> I work until the children come home—3:30 or 4 in the afternoon. If things are going well, I feel a little drugged by the events in my story; I'm desperate to know what happens next. When the children ring the doorbell I have trouble sorting my lives out. . . . I save my afternoons for them, and feel lucky to have such indisputable, ultra real ties to the everyday world; but still in those first few minutes I'm torn in two directions, and I often wonder what it would be like to live all alone in a shack by the sea and work 23 hours a day.[14]

The good news Tyler seems to derive for her own life from this book is that Mary Tell (in her manner of perception and "Telling") is an artist as well as Jeremy, that the time spent outside the study is artistically valid. The bad news is that Mary and Jeremy are not a good fit and cannot remain together, that there is a certain schizoid aspect to the writer's life. Yet, in one of the book's cannier ironies, Tyler seems to acknowledge total retreat as no possibility at all; once Jeremy, by ignoring their belated wedding day, has driven Mary and the children from the house, he pauses to rejoice in his new freedom:

> Deserted, he was like an old man who sees the last of the guests to the door and returns, stretching, and yawning, to an empty room. Now I am alone again, he says. Finally. We can get down to what I have been waiting to do.
> What is it I have been waiting to do? (169–70)

Seen through Jeremy's eyes in the sections he narrates,

13. Anne Jones observed that Mary and Jeremy can represent Tyler's own divided life in "Home at Last and Homesick Again: The Ten Novels of Anne Tyler," 5.
14. "Because I Want More than One Life."

Mary is entirely comfortable in the world. Where Jeremy cannot negotiate a walk off his own block, she repairs plumbing and pays the orthodontists. She is a monster of fecundity, filling the house with children. To Jeremy, who must process reality in tiny bits—stealing swatches of red cloth from the lining of one of his children's coats, for instance—Mary seems to engage the world fearlessly.

Mary's own sections, however, qualify this portrait by demonstrating her self-consciousness, the elements of her psyche that reveal fundamental affinities to Jeremy's even though they respond to the world in opposite ways. Tyler is careful, in other words, to construct a cognitive model for Mary's patterns of experience that has the same complexity as Jeremy's, to counter his agoraphobia with an appetite for experience. Jeremy and Mary, thus, divide more than Tyler's day. They share between them the task of constituting a portrait of the artist's contradictory desires. Jeremy is the white cubicle; Mary the longing for "more than one life." In her first narrative section, Mary remembers her life with Guy Tell:

> I would stand in front of the mirror and see how wide-hipped and expansive I was, how tall I loomed, bigger than life, *full* of life, with not enough people to pour it into. My world had turned out narrow after all—different from my parents', but just as narrow. I looked out the front window and watched the people walking by, and I wanted to climb into every single one of them and be carried off to some new and foreign existence, I pictured myself descending from the sky, all wheeling arms and legs, to sink invisibly into their heads and ride home with them, to see how they arranged their furniture and who their friends were, what they fought about, what made them cry, where they went for fun and what they ate for breakfast and how they got to sleep at night and what they dreamed of. And having found out I would leave; on to the next one. (67)

Mary Tell, then, represents the experimental consciousness an artist must have, the obverse of an equally necessary reclusion. Her final act as a narrator is her construction of a vignette in which she tells and then retells the same fairy tales to her children: "Rapunzel. The Princess and the Pea. Rumpelstiltskin. My voice grows croaky. My mind runs ahead of the words" (200). The repetition of her narration to her children calls to mind the kaleidoscope to which she compared Jeremy's art, as well as the cycle of men—Guy, John, Jeremy (and probably Brian)— with whom she lives. Tyler constructs a plot chiasmus by leaving Mary—not Jeremy—in a shack by the sea (symbol of absolute artistic solitude). If Jeremy's sculptures "grow up," Mary's children are her productions.

Surprisingly, Mary's fearlessness emerges in the novel from an initial phobic reaction. Her first erotic impulses were awakened by Guy Tell at Dewbridge Lake, where she went with her strict Baptist parents. She was frightened by Guy's skinny naked back, his roughness, and his "tacky" bathing suit (55). Her memory of that initial discovery points up the fearfulness, the fragmentariness, and the unreality of things. It is Mary, not Jeremy, who flirts with solipsism:

> Is Dewbridge Lake still there? Well, it must be. But after that one summer I have never been back. It's as if the lake had fulfilled its purpose and then vanished from the face of the earth. . . . Now I imagine that the entire forest has fallen, giving off no sound, like that tree they always bring up in science classes. All that will remain of it is a little golden dust floating upwards in the sunlight. Yet there is a thirty-nine cent strawberry-lipstick in the dimestore whose smell can still, to this day, carry me back to the ladies' changing rooms at Dewbridge Lake. Hot pine needles will always make me feel pleasantly endangered and out of my depth. The trashy taste of orange Nehi fills me even now with a longing to break loose, to go to foreign places, to try some adventure undreamed of by my father in his baggy plaid trunks and my mother in her black rayon bathing suit with the pleated skirt. (56)

Thus, Mary Tell is as problematically tied to the world as Jeremy is, but in her case it is the world that is insufficient. Her meditations on her unsettled life and its lack of vividness—despite a superficially scandalous biography—are written in diarylike form, a self-addressed inventory of experiences rather than objects. Mary finds sufficient audience in herself. Her narrative contrasts with that of Olivia, who repeatedly tries to persuade the reader, and herself, of her existence.

The four narrative sections that track Jeremy Pauling's consciousness tease out an economic aspect inherent in the book's many images of circulation. These sections establish undefinability as Jeremy's dominant characteristic and his heart's deepest need. Tyler stages two of Jeremy's panic reactions in the novel in spaces that play on the prefix *agora*, or "marketplace." Jeremy avoids markets in part because they are terrifyingly public locations but also because they signify a world that wants to define him economically. In the second of Jeremy's four sections, he attempts to leave his own block in order to follow Mary to a grocery store located a terrifying two blocks from home. As he attempts to propose marriage to Mary (a contract that would define Jeremy as husband, and in which groceries would become his inescapable responsibility), Jeremy feels his knees buckle and falls to the sidewalk. In his third section, Jeremy reluctantly agrees to visit the one-man show of his own work at Brian's gallery, where the sale of his pieces provides the main portion of his income. He panics when he sees that there are visitors examining his work.

"I want to go home, Mary," Jeremy said. He turned to find her and saw, behind her worried face, all the spectators looking pleased. Of course, they seemed to be saying, this is what we expected all along. Brian *told* us. Had he, in fact, told them something? Did Jeremy have some kind of reputation? (147–48)

In both markets—the grocery store and the art gallery—what terrifies Jeremy is the idea of being fixed, either as husband, as eccentric, or as supplier of the commodity "art." Jeremy will settle for the absence of a definable selfhood so long as it means that no selfhood is imposed upon him from outside. Marriage would likewise inscribe Jeremy in a public role as a conventional male, a provider. Thus the happy decade of his union with Mary in the boardinghouse was occasioned by the impossibility of a divorce from Guy Tell; when the divorce comes through and Mary proposes marriage, Jeremy retreats into the impenetrable privacy of his work.

Tyler reproduces Jeremy's atomistic consciousness in the narrative style of his sections, which are told in flashes and stay very close to the minute visual texture of scenes. Few generalized observations are permitted, and the segues from one section to the next are mere time references. Like Jeremy, the narrative seems to wake up and find itself, record a small epiphany, and sink back into somnolence. New sections within Jeremy's narrative typically begin with a cognitive inventory, with the formulaic opening "here is a" followed by a list. The first such inventory, of Jeremy's phobias, establishes the narrative pattern:

Summer and Fall, 1961: Jeremy

These are some of the things that Jeremy Pauling dreaded: using the telephone, answering the doorbell, opening mail, leaving his house, making purchases. Also wearing new clothes, standing in open spaces, meeting the eyes of a stranger, eating in the presence of others, turning on electrical appliances. (76)

Despite its delineation of the soul of an agoraphobe, it would be wrong to conclude that *Celestial Navigation* is a psychological novel. Tyler offers only the smallest clues (in the form of Jeremy's absent father, his reliance on maternal security, and his discomfort in the presence of men), on which to construct a psychoanalysis. Instead, what we find at the very center of the book, its sole concern for 250 pages, is Jeremy's invisibility. As with one of Jeremy's artworks, what is contained by Tyler's novel is the poignancy of absence. It tells us that portraiture is impossible, that the soul is indefinite. After Mary is gone, Miss Vinton sees Jeremy's sculpture of a young girl and says, "It's Darcy." The narrator provides Jeremy's silent reaction: "He was only modeling the people he had seen in real life, wasn't he? No. There was no way to sum people up; he was making new ones. An imaginary family" (224). Thus the poetics of agoraphobia are finally nonmimetic. The structure of *Celestial Navigation* reproduces Jeremy's need not to be defined. The six chapters narrated by characters fail to sum Jeremy up. Guests in his boardinghouse, residents in Tyler's novel, these characters come to realize, in varying degrees, that we do not know other people; we merely use them to invent fictions. In what might be called the climactic section of the novel, Jeremy, working at a driven pace to avoid thoughts of his impending wedding, all but disappears. The page contains diarylike passages of the working artist, in which Tyler in her study all but steps in for Jeremy as the center of this impossible portrait. It is a metafictional trick, and as intriguing a piece of combined self-revelation and self-concealment as the convex mirror at the center of Jan Van Eyck's *Arnolfini Marriage Group*.

Tyler has written two books that constitute a kind of poetics of illusory selfhood. Successful in *Celestial Navigation*, I think the project goes awry in *Morgan's Passing*, a novel that explores the obverse of Jeremy by creating a character who is an amalgam of Olivia's poseurship and Mary's appetite for multiple lives. *Morgan's Passing* operates on a level so narrowly aesthetic—the poetics of posing—that it abandons the psychological plausibility—or sense of discovery—of *Celestial Navigation*. It is a truly abstract novel, in which the motivation for Morgan's playing at pediatrician, Russian émigré, and frontiersman is the thinnest mention of the mystery of his father's suicide. Yet *Morgan's Passing* undoubtedly works out the same response to an initial fearfulness and urge for reclusion that we witness in *Celestial Navigation*. For example,

in one scene, Morgan, who works at a downtown hardware store owned by his father-in-law, arrives at work,
doffs his disguise of the day, and retreats to an inner
office within the haven of the store—with whose commercial end he has nothing whatever to do—and builds a
birdhouse with a special entrance that keeps out squir-
rels. The other side of imposture is the construction of
Chinese boxes of self-concealment. Thus Tyler implies
that Morgan's masquerades are necessary falsehoods that
he must establish before he can enter into the politics or
economics of human interaction. That, once he is so
disguised, he can deliver babies is an absurdity the novel
does not conquer.

V SEARCHING FOR CALEB

WHEN the insomnia plague strikes Macondo, in one of the most celebrated episodes of Gabriel García Márquez's *One Hundred Years of Solitude*, the fortune-teller Pilar Ternera discovers a new application for her skill. The citizens, as sleeplessness unstitches their memories, come to Pilar in search of the past just as they used to come in search of the future. It is not important that what she gives them is illusion. It is important that her readings constitute the past in a certain style:

> At the beginning of the road into the swamp they put up a sign that said MACONDO and another large one on the main street that said GOD EXISTS. In all the houses keys to memorizing objects and feelings had been written. But the system demanded so much vigilance and moral strength that many succumbed to the spell of an imaginary reality, one invented by themselves, which was less practical for them but more comforting. Pilar Ternera was the one who contributed most to popularize that mystification when she conceived the trick of reading the past in cards as she had read the future before. By means of that recourse the insomniacs began to live in a world built on the uncertain alternatives of the cards, where a father was remembered faintly as the dark man who had arrived at the beginning of April and a mother was remembered only as the dark woman who wore a gold ring on her left hand, and a birth date was reduced to the last Tuesday on which a lark sang in the laurel tree.[1]

Márquez's joke has become a touchstone of the new history. Our formulations of the past tend to constitute it. The past resembles the future in its refusal to tell us when our statements about it are largely exercises in convention. Anne Tyler's *Searching for Caleb* numbers a fortune-teller

---

1. *One Hundred Years of Solitude* (New York: Avon/Bard, 1970), 53–54.

among its citizens, Justine Peck. Like the inhabitants of Macondo, she is an insomniac; like Pilar Ternera, she reads cards. Also like Pilar, she finds herself applying her skills to the past instead of the future, as she accompanies her grandfather in search of his brother, who disappeared in 1912. "I read the future, not the past," she tells Alonzo Divich, because the past is "far more complicated."[2] But in the end she does read the past, finding in Caleb the key to herself.

There are other signals that Tyler is under a powerful Márquezian influence here. *Searching for Caleb* covers one hundred years, from the founding of Justin Montague Peck's import business in downtown Baltimore in the 1870s to the decision of Justine and Duncan Peck, his great-grandchildren, to join a carnival in 1973. The novel concerns the power of heredity and, like *One Hundred Years of Solitude*, defines heredity as myth—family members partially invent versions of themselves and then accept those versions as fatally imposed. Tyler's genetic comedy even repeats the Buendían instinct for endogamy, for the marriage of Duncan and Justine, who are first cousins, constitutes a final incest that results in the birth of their daughter, Megin, a monster of Peckism and the sole remaining Peck of the fourth generation. In her, and her marriage to the insipid Reverend Millsap, the Peck line dies forever. But unlike those of the Buendías, the Pecks' genes do not encode passion or mysticism but an icy, angelic conservatism of the instincts. Unlike the last of the Buendías, Meg is not born with a tail; the "House of Peck"—actually a string of four houses in Roland Park—is subject to no cleansing fire; and the family's final gasp is a wheeze of Protestantism.

Also like Márquez, Tyler structures time in her narrative after the manner of epic. *Searching for Caleb* opens in the early 1970s, as Justine helps her grandfather Daniel look for his lost brother. They ride the Amtrak to New

2. *Searching for Caleb* (New York: Berkeley Books, 1983), 41. Hereafter cited parenthetically in the text by page number.

York in pursuit of a clue, and Tyler begins the novel *in medias res* in an unnamed town in New Jersey, seen from a train window. From there the narrative opens outward to provide the history of the family from its commercial beginnings in the nineteenth century to its era of establishment, when a generation of stodgy lawyers all drove black Fords and married weak outsiders whom they molded to Peckish ways. The story then moves past its beginnings and catches up with the death of Daniel and the finding of Caleb. But, although the epic temporal arrangements of Tyler's and Márquez's novels are similar, their openings are significantly different. While Márquez's narrative flashes back to a scene in which José Aureliano faces a firing squad, Tyler repeatedly cuts to a decidedly less dramatic point, with Justine riding a train, or a bus, and offering her uncle Cheez Doodles or Ludens cough drops. Tyler's sense of what and how much is adaptable from South American magic realism to Middle Atlantic domestic comedy is nearly flawless, and John Updike was accurate in calling the book's commonplaceness both "spooky and suspenseful."[3]

It may also have been Márquez's work that suggested to Tyler the idea of defining the novel's pattern in terms of two opposed brothers, whose descendants repeat the personality traits of one or the other of them so pronouncedly that they come to define categories. Daniel and Caleb enable Tyler to perform an inquiry into the familial and more broadly cultural forces that shape both individual personality and collective history. The result is a timely expansion of her canvas. Although regional cultural aspects provided local color to *The Clock Winder,* that book considered the question of the determinative power

3. "Family Ways." This review is reprinted in *Hugging the Shore,* 273–78. This quotation appears on 276. Updike complains of Southern Gothic gimmickry in Tyler's hiding Caleb's secret with Sulie Boudrault, the family's black maid, for sixty years. Also, the unexplained infertility of Justine and Duncan's four other cousins, in order to make Megin the last of the Pecks, sags under a weight of schematicism.

of family alone. *Searching for Caleb* provides a referentiality to the term *Peck*, making the family a window rather than a wall. Typically, in earlier Tyler novels the subject was family and the time frame was a decade (rather precisely a decade in *Celestial Navigation* and *The Clock Winder*). In *Searching for Caleb,* the time frame is a century and the subject is not just the heritability of Peckism but its cultural signification. Clearly, the Pecks continue those traits I have previously termed *agoraphobic*. They remain housebound, and they fear strangers. But in *Searching for Caleb* these traits are given a context in American society; the "agora"—the market—is the place the Peck men leave for and return from but which is not allowed to corrupt the serenity of their homes.[4] (Guano is one untidy source of the Peck wealth.)

Admittedly, there is a tentativeness in the way Tyler's fascination with agoraphobia leads her into social history. She traces the Peck family origins only as far back as Justin Montague Peck, who established his import business sometime in the 1870s and built the first two houses in Roland Park. Probably because Tyler wants to tie off narrative strings, Justin remains a sociological enigma. His first and middle names are typically white Anglo-Saxon, but the novel is deliberately obscure about the ethnic origin of *Peck* and denies the reader knowledge that surely Justin's son Daniel would have possessed:

> Duncan and Justine Peck shared a great-grandfather named Justin Montague Peck, a sharp-eyed, humorless man who became very rich importing coffee, sugar, and guano during the last quarter of the nineteenth century. On any

4. See Gillian Brown, "The Empire of Agoraphobia," *Representations* 20 (Fall 1987): 134–57. Brown argues for the functionality of agoraphobia in placing the female citizens of a free market economy on pedestals. The consequent separation of market and home allowed a double standard that ensured the survival of the Victorian ideal of the home presided over by a "pure" woman. Tyler's portrayal of the Peck women, especially Caroline, Justine's baby-doll mother, is quite compatible with Brown's account.

summer day in the 1870's, say, you could find him seated in the old Merchants' Exchange on Gay Street, smoking one of his long black cigars to ward off yellow fever, waiting for news of his ships to be relayed from the lookout tower on Federal Hill. Where he originally came from was uncertain, but the richer he grew the less it mattered. Although he was never welcomed into Baltimore society, which was narrow and ossified even then, he was treated with respect and men often asked his advice on financial issues. (53)

The picture matches rather well with E. Digby Baltzell's account of the Jewish investment banker Sidney Weinberg, who was a "personal friend" of numerous WASP establishment figures but was never invited to their clubs.[5] (As J. P. Morgan put it, "Do business with anyone, but only sail with a gentleman.") Tyler portrays Baltimore in the late nineteenth century as having an aristocracy that, in the terms of Baltzell's analysis, has degenerated into a caste. What she does not provide are the specifics of Justin Montague Peck's exclusion, or why he in turn sired a family that made exclusion a first principle. But she does not entirely sidestep the problem, either. Here is young Duncan's version of it:

"What's so uncommon about us? We're not famous, we're not society, we haven't been rich since 1930 and we aren't known for brains or beauty. But our ladies wear hats, by God! And we all have perfect manners! We may not ever talk to outsiders about anything more interesting than the weather, but at least we do it politely! And we've all been taught that we disapprove of sports cars, golf, women in slacks, chewing gum, the color chartreuse, emotional displays, ranch houses, bridge, mascara, household pets, religious discussions, plastic, politics, nail polish, transparent gems of any color, jewelry shaped like animals, checkered prints. . . . we write our bread and butter notes no more than an hour after every visit . . . we always say 'Baltimore' instead of 'Balmer' . . . even when we're wearing our ragged old gardening clothes you

5. *The Protestant Establishment: Aristocracy and Caste in America* (New York, Random House, 1963), 36.

can peek down our collars and see 'Brooks Brothers' on the label, and our boots are English and meant for riding though none of us has ever sat on a horse." (93)

When agoraphobia conjoins with a historical impulse, the result is reticent history. The Pecks are standoffish, but they reveal no ugly ethnic or racial prejudices. They are xenophobic, but we do not see them with foreigners, only with other Pecks. Tyler delimits their social referentiality, but it is there; except for grandfather Justin's *arriviste* status, they fit the historical mold of the eastern WASP establishment that Baltzell profiles so tellingly. Here, for instance, is his citation of the testimony of T. S. Matthews, the heir to Proctor and Gamble and the managing editor of *Time* in the 1950s:

> From early childhood, Matthews was bred in the defensive atmosphere which is still characteristic of the American rich, and which only emphasized his sense of difference from other people in the world about him. Thus he writes of his childhood in Cincinnati: "The nursery was the heart of our world and our refuge from the rest of it. . . . The front door was not only latched but bolted . . . the parlormaid's nightly duty was to draw the curtains in all the windows that gaze on the street, and also to shut and latch the shutters. . . . The fact that we were different was never absent from our consciousness. We were ashamed of our timidity and our lack of sturdiness, but we despised the rest of the world for all that, and looked down on everybody that was not like us. And we were sure that nobody *was* like us."[6]

Peckism is not merely a Tylerian fantasy; it is a significant fact of American commercial life.

Justin Montague Peck has two sons by two mothers. Daniel, the firstborn, is the child of Sarah Cantleigh, Justin's first wife, and he grows up to inherit his father's conservative instincts. Caleb is the child of Laura Baum,

6. Ibid., 40–41.

Justin's second wife, and he inherits the Baums' wanderlust and their love of music.

Daniel represents that side of the human community that loves order, dwells in cities, establishes legal codes, and walls out those forces in nature that are seen as unruly, barbarian, and autochthonous. He is, in short, a representative of *homo cultus, homo civis,* a man of culture, a man of civility. And Baltimore is his civil polity.

It is significant that Daniel and the other members of his generation of Pecks practice law, a form of conflict ritualized into solemn game. They bring home from their profession a language that is formal, polite, and cunning in its self-exoneration. Indirect and ambiguous, their words leave the onus of guilt upon the outsider. Duncan rages against his mother, who has become a Peck by marriage: "She's just like all the rest of them now. Too little said and too much communicated, so that if you fight back they can say, 'But why? What did *I* do?' and you won't have an answer. It all takes place in their secret language, they would never say a thing straight out" (98). Pecks are definers of, and dwellers inside, the pale. When a Peck does go visiting, he or she carries pen and paper in order to write and mail a thank-you note on the way home. This note mentions and praises some specific item on the dinner table. Pecks are comfortable believing that one evokes the item in order to establish that the letter was written after the visit, not before, although they see nothing inherently wrong with that alternative. The bread-and-butter letter fulfills a duty and discharges guilt; it never risks emotional directness yet allows its recipient to interpret it in a number of ways that may constitute rebuke. Far more than saying thank you, it negotiates a separation.

In one scene, Daniel Peck, the ninety-three-year-old champion of the family's polite aloofness, attends a Quaker meeting and asks Justine to rise and read his definition of heaven:

"My grandfather wants me to read this," she said. " 'I used to

95

think that heaven was—palatable? Palatial. I was told it had pearly gates and was paved with gold. But now I hope they are wrong about that. I would prefer to find that heaven was a small town with a bandstand in the park and a great many trees, and I would know everybody in it and none of them would ever die or move away or age or alter.' " (198)

This is not really a theological vision, it is a utopia—a figment of secular imagining, a civic order of granite inalterability. And it contains the seeds of its own destruction in the nostalgic impulse that lies behind its sentimental imagery. For wound about Daniel's hatred of change is his longing for his brother, who wandered off one summer afternoon in 1912. In a lifetime that has had little room for emotion, nostalgia—disguised as a conviction of the rightness of his life—has lingered, becoming the one feeling that will undo Daniel. Caleb has come to represent to him his own life lived in the contrary-to-fact subjunctive—choices not made, emotions denied. Glimmers of his error come to Daniel in the last months of his life: "In my childhood I was trained to hold things in, you see. But I thought I was holding them in until a certain *time*. I assumed that someday, somewhere, I would again be given the opportunity to spend all that saved-up feeling. When will that be?" (258–59). Nonetheless, once he locates Caleb, Daniel cannot resist an urge to rebuke him, and he does so in a wonderfully sad, uninsightful letter. What Daniel can barely stand to learn is that he has constructed Caleb as an anti-self, a haunting alternative. Self-conceived as a bringer of civic light, Daniel dies obsessed with a shadow.

Tyler's temporal cutting and pasting in *Searching for Caleb* provides an interesting complication upon the genetic novel: on one side of the fraternal antithesis, she provides a repetition of the pattern before introducing the original. Thus, the reader meets Caleb's great-nephew, Duncan, a repetition of the Caleb type, an anti-Peck, before Caleb is introduced, in fact before it is even clear to the reader that he is alive.

In Duncan's rebellion, Peckism appears as a long-established—and therefore much to be resented—system. From his earliest youth, Duncan gestured at leaving the pale. The imagery in which Tyler presents his life's project sheds light on the cultural dimension of the Pecks as significant American types. When Duncan is a boy, he climbs trees; ordered down from them, he hangs from his ankles and lands on his head. The trees playfully mark Duncan as *homo silvestris* (he is like Italo Calvino's Cosimo in *Baron in the Trees* in his passionate rebellion against all the values that the family estate embodies). He despises the city of Baltimore, and he hates the law. The Pecks are steady; he is a leaf on the crosswinds of his own enthusiasms. The Pecks are sober; when one of his enthusiasms wanes, Duncan drinks bourbon. The Pecks are sexually repressed and wary of outsiders; Duncan brings home a girl of a lower social station who wears a red dress. (But then he seduces and marries his own cousin, Justine, an act that causes more delight than outrage, since it means no new daughter-in-law for the Pecks to get used to.) Duncan devours Dostoyevsky, moves into a garret above a bookstore, and contemplates going mad. It is there that Justine, sent as a delegation by the family, falls in love with him because of his oppositeness—an irony in that the love affair ends in the endogamy Duncan must logically abhor.

As anti-Peck, Duncan will accept neither a permanent residence nor a steady means of employment. The houses he and Justine move into are flimsy, made of paper, lacking the substance of the Roland Park estates. At the novel's end, Duncan and Justine, having found and lost Caleb and with their grandfather dead, drive away from their neighbors to take up residence in a carnival trailer. Duncan's work invariably constitutes a text which he invites the other members of his family to read as an inversion of their principles. Duncan and Justine first take up goatherding, a nomadic employment. Later, Duncan agrees to sell antiques, but he refuses to handle furniture, a mainstay of Peck substantiality, and sells only old tools, which remind him of the inventiveness of the American nineteenth century. Duncan's love of machines echoes that of José Arcadio Buendía in its magical aspect. It inverts the Pecks' practicality, for he dreams only of impossible things: perpetual-motion devices and one-man airplanes smaller than chairs. While working at the antique store, Duncan decides to grow corn in the front yard of the rented house in which he and Justine are living and to fertilize it with garbage that he has put through the blender. Duncan's attempts at subsistence living fail, but they do not need to succeed, only to outrage. Unfortunately, Duncan's rebellion ultimately brings not freedom but entrapment inside a round of antifamilial gestures.

Caleb, as the originator of the alternative to Peckism, was never so self-conscious, or so condemned to futile gestures. There is innocence in first times around. One of the pleasures of the novel is the order in which the facts about Caleb are discovered, the way in which they provide a musical counterpointing to the character of Duncan. These facts emerge from Daniel's troubled memories, and then from the investigations of the private detective Eli Everjohn (who looks like Abraham Lincoln and strives to restore union between divided brothers—another link to the "American" theme).

Caleb, from his boyhood, loved music, popular rather than classical. To him a street musician was a pied piper, to be followed into the remotest sections of Baltimore. The family would follow the music to find him and fetch him home. Justin Montague despised the gypsy soul in Caleb; when Caleb announced his choice of a musical profession over a place in the family import business, Justin suffered a stroke and lost the use of the left side of his body. When he tried to denounce Caleb, "all that came from his mouth were strange vowel sounds" (57). Like Mrs. Emerson in *The Clock Winder,* he has lost his power of speech and thus his ability to criticize his son. With his father unable to speak, Caleb's mother fills in, rebuking him with the stunning line, "You have killed your half of your father." This is a brilliant moment of realist characterization; it is also schematic. From this moment, Peckism is bisected into the earnest stay-at-homes and the drifters, and one-half of Justin's stolidity has melted away with the muscle tone on the left side of his face. Caleb guiltily stays with the business for another decade, until his father's death. Then, one summer afternoon in 1912, he walks away.

It is Eli Everjohn who, sixty-one years later, uncovers his whereabouts and his history: Caleb, admiring the piano playing of the Creole family gardener, LaFleur Boudrault, had slid southward to New Orleans, where he hooked up with a blind, black blues singer named White Eye. In order to avoid losing each other, Caleb and White Eye stayed tied together by a rope—thus Caleb's renaming as "the stringtail man." Homeless, adrift, and moderately happy, Caleb thus reestablished union and brotherhood on his own democratic terms, far outside his family's xenophobia. Yet he and White Eye were never good friends and hardly spoke. It was in the rhythms and tonalities of their music that they were united. White Eye died, Caleb's fingers grew too stiff for fiddling, and he moseyed through a series of relationships and jobs, including short-order cook, finally winding up in a state home for the elderly and indigent where music was forbidden. After her grandfather's heart attack, Justine, trying to fill an aching absence, brings Caleb home, but he is uncomfortable back inside even her jerry-built outpost of the pale. He escapes one night, and Justine receives a letter from Wyoming:

November 20, 1973

Dear Justine,

I want to apologize for taking so long to write, but circumstances prevented me up until now.

It was very kind of you to invite me to stay with you. The frankfurters you cooked were delicious, and I shall remember my visit with a great deal of pleasure for a long time to come.

Love,
Caleb Peck (314)

The letter, and Caleb's existence, surprisingly, does not set Duncan free from his compulsive gesturing. He remains at the novel's end largely trapped in his own evasions, still hankering after a magic that is not grounded in emotion. Rather, in the novel's logic, it is Justine for whom Caleb provides recognitions. Like the faith healer Susannah Spright in "Half-Truths and Semi-Miracles," Justine is empowered; she is the novel's witness, the one who comprehends her grandfather's late but plausible blossoming into wisdom, the pattern behind her husband's fits of enthusiasm and boredom, and her daughter's deathly need for stability. Her witnessing authenticates the lives of the people she loves.

Tyler is careful to connect Justine's fortune-telling to the alertness a novelist needs, a negative capability, the clairvoyance that in her fiction often accompanies agoraphobia, the mind vivified in retreat. Born with an intuitive ability to sense change, Justine visits Madame Olita, who identifies her as an authentic fortune-teller and teaches her the use of cards:

"No, You must think of these cards as tags."

"Tags," Justine said blankly.

"Tags with strings attached, like those surprise boxes at parties. The strings lead into your mind. These cards will pull out what you already know, but have failed to admit or recognize." (136)

She tells Justine that only those—like her—who lead a still life can feel the motions in the lives of others. Justine turns to Madame Olita because she shares Elizabeth Abbot's need to evade responsibility. If fortunes can be foretold, can they be altered? Because her marriage with Duncan has precipitated the fatal heart attack of her father and the suicide of her mother, Justine has traveled to downtown Baltimore for secular absolution. She goes

100

to the dry cleaner's where Madame Olita used to have her parlor and talks to the owner. He tells her he consults fortune-tellers for one reason only:

> "Say you got a problem, some decision to make. You ask your minister. You ask your psychiatrist, psychologist, marriage counselor, lawyer—they all say, 'Well of course I can't decide *for* you and we want to look at all the angles here and I wouldn't want to be responsible for—' They hedge their bets you see. But not Madame Olita. Not *any* good fortune teller. 'Do X,' they say. 'Forget Y.' 'Stop seeing Z.' It's wonderful, they take full responsibility. What more could we ask?" (132)

When she becomes a fortune-teller, Justine does not drop her own burdens, she picks up those of her customers. The visit with Madame Olita, now dying, only compounds things. Madame Olita tells her: "You can change your future a great deal. Also your past. . . . Not what happened, no, but what hold it has on you" (135). In effect, that is the lesson of Justine's search for Caleb. Justine learns from him what hold the past has on herself, and on Duncan and Megin, and how much of it is self-imposed.

Justine's absence of self and her wide-eyed perceptiveness make her an able witness of the lives of the people among whom she and Duncan live when they exile themselves from the Peckian Eden. A considerable amount of the novel's attention goes to recording the blowsy insouciance of the lower-middle-class people whom Justine befriends, the same type of people whom Tyler will celebrate in all the characters of *Earthly Possessions* and in the residents of Muriel's block of row houses in that magical working-class section of Baltimore where Macon Leary finds refuge in *The Accidental Tourist*.

These characters constitute one-half of the people Tyler writes about (the other half are members of the mercantile upper middle class, like the Pecks). They began as North Carolinians of a dour disposition and an acute sense of limited possibility in *The Tin Can Tree* and *A Slipping-Down*

101

Life; then, when Tyler's imagination moved north, they became bumptious lower-middle-class people with double names like Anne-Campbell and Joe-Pete (Justine and Duncan's Caro Mill neighbors). These people occupy a planet with very little gravitational pull. They get married, then divorced, then remarried, often to their first spouses. Their hearts direct them. They represent, in Walter Kaiser's terms, *physis* over *nomos*, bodily instinct over intellectual law, spontaneity over prudence.[7] Thus, in Tyler's schematic, they are connected to things like fortune-telling because it represents an intuitive response to the random, a liberating sense of one's own eccentricity and even unimportance. Yet they—unlike the Pecks— have lives that form into stories. Culturally, they are inscribed in Tyler's fiction as readers of magazines like the *National Enquirer* and watchers of soap operas; as eaters of irregular and unbalanced meals; as wearers of garish, cheap, sexy clothes, who sit guiltlessly idle in midday, munching on chocolates. As family members, they are impolite and squabble in front of neighbors with bluntness and tenacity. They make up the unstable communities into which Duncan and Justine drop each time they arrive in a new town.

These are the people who form an America that Tyler has allowed her upper-middle-class characters to look at through windows, to envy, and even to yearn for. In fact, almost every Tyler novel chronicles the self-exile of someone of upper-middle-class background among the lower middle class. Her admiration for the relatively poor has been largely unmixed; until *The Accidental Tourist,* she has charmed or kidded away the darker side of economic insufficiency. The freedom of the anti-Pecks (Caleb, Duncan, and Justine) rests on their immersion in this social stratum, even if that immersion is not taken entirely seriously. The trust fund that Justine and Duncan inherited from Justin Montague Peck is the novelist's honest

7. See Kaiser's *Praisers of Folly* (Cambridge: Harvard University Press, 1963), 53.

acknowledgment that money cushions Pecks against real exigencies, even away from home. This changes after *Searching for Caleb*. With Pearl Tull and Muriel Pritchett, Tyler fully imagines the pain that is also part of social inconsequence. Poorer characters are seen from a more intimate angle; the window is gone. But in earlier novels, shortness of money, loss of health, and emotional turmoil are treated as pastoral conditions; Tyler is not quite guilty of sentimentality, but her vision is certainly limited to the comic registers. Until about 1980, hardship for Tyler's characters represented little more than an opportunity to display their gift of insouciance.

This problem is most acute in the character of Duncan. In the end, his critique of the exclusivism of his family is futile, and he is unable to break the stifling pattern of caste that Tyler seems to want the family's behavior to signify. In Baltzell's terms, Duncan is that sad thing, an alienated aristocrat, whose bitterness does not carry him to a vital democratism but to a kind of calcified childhood. Duncan's subject will never be America, it will always be Pecks.

Justine fares better. The final irony of the novel—when she meets her Uncle Caleb and takes him in—is that she does not like him. His street music is inscribed as a thing of real democratic worth. His escape is to a real freedom, not a life of empty gestures. He embodies what Updike called "the lyrical, mystical irrational underside of American practicality."[8] But Justine cannot take direction from him. He is too passive. He accepts all invitations, even Justine's to go home with her. The search for Caleb was a search for herself, and its success is sardonic. At the center of Caleb—to the extent that he has one—is the emptiness he shares with Justine.

Caleb teaches Justine something. Her gypsy life with Duncan was not a response to the waywardness of her own heart; she would have been happy to stay at home with the Pecks forever. She followed Duncan out of the

8. See "Family Ways," in *Hugging the Shore*, 276.

103

same agreeableness that caused Caleb to come home with her. But as nomadism becomes second nature to her, Duncan sometimes "remembered that she had not always been this way, though he couldn't put his finger on just when she had changed. Then he wondered if she only *pretended* to be happy, for his sake. Or if she were deliberately cutting across her own grain, like an acrophobe who takes up sky diving" (153). But Justine scarcely has a grain. In her childhood, she longed to be a Peck, to enjoy membership, to be a link in a network. As an adult, she agrees with whoever is talking; she mirrors the person she is with. Her "curse," Duncan knows, is to "see all sides." What he also knows, and cannot possibly admit, is that she stays with him because he is a Peck, and with him she is by definition home and safe.

The artistry of *Searching for Caleb* carries Tyler's inventory technique to its high-water mark; in subsequent novels she uses less density of material detail, increasingly willing to drop the brush for the palette knife. In a way Jeremy's sculptures remain the aptest metaphor for the narrative techniques of *Searching for Caleb*. First, there is junk; Tyler piles it in front of us, obstructing our steps and our view. When Justine and Duncan move, for instance, it takes them twice as long to carry in their boxes of assorted broken lamp parts as it does their furniture. But Duncan may want to invent something from all this detritus. One of Tyler's favorite terms for her work, *kaleidoscope*, recurs in this novel as an attribute of Justine's personality. *Searching for Caleb* is a kaleidoscope in the sense that the earlier novels are: it makes patterns out of what seem like thousands of bits of information about character, from favorite armchairs to pet obsessions. But *Searching for Caleb* achieves a deliberate redundancy of information, linking so many traits of one character to so many traits of others that one finally despairs of interpretation. The book has a richness that produces the illusion of infinity, an inexhaustible series of permutations. One can pick any object or event and run it through the novel, tracing a series of kaleidoscopic patterns that suggest to the reader that there are only bits of glass at the end of the tube. This is a postmodern trick whose effect is to confound the simplifications of past and future that Pilar Ternera imposes on her clients. To despair of interpretation is to find freedom of change and choice.

Thus, it is finally not only Caleb whom the novel is missing. Late in the book, after Caleb is gone again, Justine dreams that she is in a lighthouse, considering it as a possible next residence, when she wakes up and thinks that all her life has been an incoherent rush at the future. "And Justine awoke one day to wonder how it had happened: what she had mislaid was Justine herself" (266). But no sentence about the self is ever final in this book, and all patterns are imposed. That is the source of what Updike called the "spooky" aspect of *Searching for Caleb*. What Tyler would defend about the novel is its warmth. Caleb and Justine's capacity for love—the honest, unfrightened expression of it—redeems them, even if they are just bits of glass.

WITH *Earthly Possessions*, Anne Tyler abandoned the densely textured, kaleidoscopic narratives of her previous three novels and experimented instead with a more bumptious manner of telling. She replaced the unobtrusive, omniscient voice that patiently reported the surface worlds of *The Clock Winder, Celestial Navigation*, and *Searching for Caleb* with an idiosyncratic first-person narrator. *Earthly Possessions* has a sudden, slapdash surface that disguises what is assuredly Tyler's most thoroughly schematic conception. In 222 pages, Charlotte Emory tells two stories. The first (contained in the book's odd-numbered chapters) reports her attempt to leave her husband. She goes to the bank to withdraw her savings and is kidnapped by a bank robber, Jake Simms, who takes her south as a hostage in a stolen car. In Georgia, they pick up his seventeen-year-old pregnant girlfriend, Mindy Callendar. Then, in Florida, Charlotte walks away from Jake and his gun and goes home. The second story (told in the even-numbered chapters) is Charlotte's autobiography, an act of retrospection occasioned by the flight to Florida, a defining of the "home" she tried to leave. It carries Charlotte from her birth in 1941 (she is Tyler's age exactly) in Clarion, Maryland, through an odd and lonely childhood as the daughter of a depressive portrait photographer and an obese agoraphobic mother, then on to marriage to the hellfire preacher Saul Emory and the inexorable accumulation of people and things that finally drove her to run. The end of the story told in the even-numbered chapters—in which Charlotte opens a cereal box and finds an omen in the "keep on truckin'" badge that spills out—is the beginning of the story told in the odd-numbered chapters, so that the narrative structure is as circular as Charlotte's flight to Florida and subsequent return home.

A casual reading tends to magnify the journey half of

the narrative.[1] In subsequent readings, the autobiography deepens, its colors become more saturated, and a pattern emerges that approaches Faulkner in the complexity of its exposition. *Earthly Possessions* is Tyler's closest brush with modernism; it half-conceals a geometry beneath its fluid surface. To describe that geometry, it is necessary to consider the autobiographical chapters first.

The first fact the reader of *Earthly Possessions* is asked to grasp is that Charlotte Emory's mother was fat. Charlotte persuades us of that the way Dickens in *A Christmas Carol* persuades us that Marley is dead. Here are the opening words of chapter 2, the beginning of the autobiographical narrative:

> I was born right here in Clarion; I grew up in that big brown turreted house next to Percy's Texaco. My mother was a fat lady who used to teach first grade. Her maiden name was Lacey Debney.
> Notice that I mention her fatness first. You couldn't overlook fatness like my mother's. It defined her, it radiated from her, it filled any room she walked into. She was a mushroom-shaped woman with wispy blond hair you could see through, a pink face, and no neck; just a jaw sloping wider and wider till it turned into shoulders.[2]

Tyler has written about the novelist's duty to sympathize, and she has confessed that she tends to emulate Eudora Welty rather than Flannery O'Connor because Welty is kinder to her characters.[3] Generally Tyler adheres rigor-

1. In fact, Roger Sale in his review of the novel decided that a good story, entitled "Jake and Charlotte," got buried in extraneous retrospection. See "Hostages," *New York Review of Books,* 26 May 1977, 39–42.

2. *Earthly Possessions* (New York: Berkeley Books, 1984), 11. Hereafter cited parenthetically in the text by page number.

3. In "The Fine Full World of Welty," D7. This was Tyler's review of the 1980 Harcourt Brace Jovanovich edition of the *Collected Stories of Eudora Welty.* Welty does imagine utterly unsympathetic people. John Updike observed, in his review of *Searching for Caleb,* that Tyler displays "a clinical benevolence not present in the comparable talent of, say, the

ously to this principle and strives to see every action from the inside. Her work has deepened in consequence, and her recent fiction, from *Dinner at the Homesick Restaurant* to *Breathing Lessons,* shows the results of this disciplining of the imagination in the form of a Shakespearian power of negative capability. But Tyler cannot live inside everyone—she draws the line at fat ladies. They mark the limit of her patience and are, therefore, instructive.

Clearly, it is fair to see Charlotte's mother, rendered in that deadpan voice of Charlotte's, as an instance of Southern grotesque. Charlotte's mother was so fat that only a patio chair could support her, and the family had to take it along in the back of a pickup on rare outings. She mistook her only pregnancy for a tumor, and Charlotte's birth came as a complete surprise. An agoraphobe, she lumbers from chairback to kitchen counter inside a house smelling of ancient, unmoving air. Her presence through most of the novel is felt as a ponderous emotional weight.

Tyler started doing studies for this particular portrait early, and with enthusiasm. The first instance is in a story titled "I'm Not Going to Ask You Again." There is ample evidence that the story is a study in Weltian themes: it concerns a piano teacher's fondness for and loss of a prize student, a recapitulation of Miss Eckhart's love for Virgie Rainey in Welty's "June Recital." Here, though, the teacher is obese—or, more accurately, she *used* to be, but has since withered some. The story tells how Noona, the teacher, attempts to go to the baseball park and explain to her prize cello student, Paul Harberg, a boy who longs for normality, that, despite appearances, it is not her intention to imprison him in her vicarious ambitions for his musical career. She fails to speak, experiences an agoraphobic panic in the park, and lumbers home in a sadly comic fashion. Here is Tyler's account of Noona's glance in a mirror:

young Eudora Welty, whose provincial characters were captured with a certain malicious pounce." "Family Ways," in *Hugging the Shore,* 278.

She rarely looked in mirrors. She had been fat from birth almost, once so fat that people had gaped at her unbelievingly and she had not dared to try to enter the narrow folding doors of city buses. Now most of the weight was gone, starved away a few years ago when the doctors had insisted, but her skin had lost its elasticity by then and had never tightened up again. The skin hanging from her upper arms could be wrapped around her arms like sleeves; it swung from her bones gently when she demonstrated a passage on the piano, causing her students to stare round-eyed.[4]

As Noona runs home, children on the sidewalk watch her and laugh. The situation of a young watcher and a fleshy older woman seems to be a conscious variant on another story by Welty entitled "A Memory," which Tyler later singled out for praise, perhaps because it concerns an agoraphobic witnessing of the world. Welty's story concerns the coming to awareness of a young girl whom Tyler described as "constructing for herself, with infinite care, a small circle of protection against the ugly and pathetic outside world."[5] The story concerns the girl's confrontation with the facts of mortal flesh as she watches a family on a lakeside beach. A man pours sand over the legs, and then between the breasts, of an obese middle-aged woman, thus connecting flesh and earth in the young watcher's mind. Here is the girl's vision of the woman on the beach: "She was unnaturally white and fatly aware, in a bathing suit which had no relation to the shape of her body. Fat hung upon her arms like an arrested earthslide on a hill. With the first motion she might make, I was afraid that she would slide down upon herself into a terrifying heap. Her breasts hung heavy and widening like pears into her bathing suit."[6] In her own story, Tyler softens the grotesquery, shifts the narrative point of view from the watch-

4. "I'm Not Going to Ask You Again," 89.

5. "The Fine Full World of Welty," D2.

6. Eudora Welty, *Collected Stories of Eudora Welty* (New York: Harcourt Brace Jovanovich, 1980), 78.

ing child to Noona, and admittedly provides her with a degree of sympathy, despite her desire to entrap.

Another early Tyler story, however, admits no sympathy where flesh has turned mountainous. "The Common Courtesies" is a word-photograph of a fat woman on her front porch. Miss Lorna is the daughter of the town's richest man, but she has retreated from her musical girlhood to a housebound, complaining middle age. When she learns that her married daughter Melissa has taken the foolish and dangerous action of becoming pregnant, she takes up a permanent defensive posture in a large and slowly collapsing wicker chair, where her housekeeper feeds her cookies:

> All during May, Miss Lorna sat on her front porch eating vanilla wafers. She kept the package in her lap, and while her fingers fumbled through the cellophane, she stared straight ahead, unblinking, watching the cars that slipped past the house. Her face was the kind that had melted with age. It ran in downward lines toward her triple chin, and the sheer weight of her body seemed to drag at the corners of her mouth and at her eyes, which were small brown points behind tunnels of webbed skin.[7]

Once again, there is a self-conscious derivativeness here. If this were a pencil drawing, it could be titled "Fat Woman, after O'Connor," for it very specifically echoes the unforgettable vision of the countrywoman Mrs. Shortley that opens "The Displaced Person":

> Her arms were folded and as she mounted the prominence, she might have been the giant wife of the countryside, come out at some sign of danger to see what the trouble was. She stood on two tremendous legs, with the grand self-confidence of a mountain, and rose, up narrowing bulges of

7. "The Common Courtesies," 62.

granite, to two icy blue points of light that pierced forward, surveying everything.[8]

Exchange xenophobia for agoraphobia, granite for mud, and O'Connor's Mrs. Shortley becomes Tyler's Lorna.

But why these portraits in the manner of Welty and O'Connor? What is it about fat women that turns one of the kindest imaginations in contemporary fiction to such relative cruelty? In all the instances I have cited—Charlotte's mother, Noona, and Lorna—fatness is a physical manifestation of the character's demands upon a child, in two cases her own, in the third a pupil. Fat is the palpable signifier of these women's dependency, their willingness to smother. The merging of flesh and world in the idea of burdensomeness is the subject of *Earthly Possessions*. It signals the one human posture that is intolerable to Tyler; she expels from the wide circle of her sympathy those who lack the moral intelligence to see that they are denying air to others. As banal forms of the parental burden, these characters provide Tyler an opportunity to demythologize the Southern theme of inherited guilt. As the early novels have demonstrated, the wicked patriarch as an Old Testament archetype has no metaphysical status in Tyler's fiction. She denies the demonic. Fathers are absent, and that absence does mark a world without authority, but the lack is a result of the fathers' incompetence. Mothers are reduced to domestic and personal forces in the guilt they inflict. In Tyler, what is inheritable is by definition mundane. Thus, *Earthly Possessions* is a return to Southern modes of writing via parody. Tyler employs the power of the grotesque to cancel metaphysical implications.

The root of Tyler's quarrel with O'Connor is original sin. In O'Connor, the grotesqueness of any human being is the measure of how far his back is turned on God. On

8. Flannery O'Connor, "The Displaced Person," in *A Good Man Is Hard to Find and Other Stories* (New York: Harcourt Brace Jovanovich, 1976), 96.

the other hand, John Updike, in a review of *Morgan's Passing*, observed a degree of restraint in Tyler's use of the grotesque. He wrote, "This is O'Connor cartooning without the cruelty, without the pinpoint tunnel to Jesus at the end of all perspectives."[9] *Morgan's Passing* is bland. *Earthly Possessions*, on the contrary, has some cruelty, and it denies that there is a tunnel, that perspectives have an end. It is finally an anti-Christian book, one that picks up O'Connor's tools with a saboteur's intent.

One O'Connor tool that Tyler picks up is cartooning. The background texture of *Earthly Possessions* continually invokes a funny-paper world: "Peanuts," "Batman," the old "Dutch Cleanser" ad, the "keep on truckin'" badge that seals Charlotte's fate. Tyler draws women as mudslides; she makes a street in a Maryland town look like a "Sesame Street" set. The car of Jake the bank robber is a balloon-like 1953 model; it loses bumpers, backs into parked cars, crashes into wheat fields. Then, in the next odd-numbered chapter, it starts up fresh again, like a mechanical Wile E. Coyote. Jake's girlfriend, Mindy, dresses with a pink heart motif and wears strawberry and sugar perfume. Her childish, saccharine cartoon surface is ironically undercut by the weight of her pregnant belly and by her backache pains, which radiate sympathetically through Charlotte to the reader. Saul Emory's brother Julian offers a paradigm of Tyler's imaginative method in the novel, its combining of fantasy and banal physicality. Julian spent time in prison, and he remembers: "I got to know a few of the prisoners. . . . Know how they passed the time? They'd chew up their bread and make it into statues, get the guards to sell it outside. . . . Little statues of Donald Duck, Minnie Mouse, people like that. Little chewed up statues" (121).

Subsequent novels have sustained this boldness of depiction—the hardness of outline, the swiftly painted impression, the goofy two-dimensionality that Tyler taught herself in the short stories and first applied to a longer

9. *New Yorker,* 23 June 1980, 101.

narrative here. The most wonderfully memorable moments in her best fiction to date possess a cartoonish quality: Macon Leary on the basement stairs, Cody Tull shooting his mother with the bow and arrow, Serena Gill replaying their wedding at Max's funeral. They go to the essential with the suddenness of caricature.

Primarily, *Earthly Possessions* focuses its satirical force upon the sacrosanct idea of "home." A conventional, Southern Christian reverence for the moral virtue of domestic stability gives the book its historical subject. Buried in Charlotte's autobiography are the stories of the decline of her own ancestral home and the decline and fall of the house of her husband, Saul Emory, who grew up across the street. In relocating the Southern myth of the ancestral house to a familiar, demotic context, Tyler succeeds in defining "earthly possessions" as the three things that weigh Charlotte down: mother, husband, and house.

Charlotte's house—a turreted place next to a Texaco station—recalls Emily Grierson's in Faulkner's "Rose for Emily," which stood near a cotton gin of more recent construction. In both cases, the gracious dwelling of the past has succumbed to a modern commercial encroachment. Charlotte looks out upon her block, where no other residence remains, and thinks, "Everyone else had moved on, and left us stranded here between the Amoco and the Texaco" (206). Lacey Debney, Charlotte's mother, was the daughter of an important state politician who was the friend of a former governor; as a girl she had played hostess at prominent social affairs. When her father died, she, like Emily Grierson, went into reclusion behind her curtains. She then married a diminutive man who opened a photography studio on the ground floor. In the intensity of her adolescence, Charlotte deeply needs to escape the closed-down, agoraphobic life of her parents, the burden her aging mother places upon her. "I knew the picture we made: fat mother in elastic stockings, shriveled father, sullen spinster daughter. House where everything was mislaid under something else, and bats were surely hanging in the turret" (64). Charlotte is blithely

113

impervious to that Southern sense of nostalgia that pervades "A Rose for Emily." To her, "home" is stagnation.

Saul's house—equally decayed—is the emotional negative of Charlotte's. It is a monument to mobility. While Charlotte's mother never left home, Saul's mother, Alberta, was a rootless woman, a gypsy who eventually abandoned her husband—a shiftless drinker—and ran off with his father. (There is a comical vestige of the Gothic theme of incest here.) Alberta's four sons deeply resented their mother:

> Their mother had been pushy, clamorous, violent, taking over their lives, meddling in their brains, demanding a constant torrent of admiration and gaiety. Her sons had winced when she burst into their rooms. She breathed her hot breath on them, she laughed her harsh laugh. She called for parties! dancing! Let's show a little *life* here! Given anything less than what she needed . . . she turned mocking and contemptuous. She had a tongue like a knife. The sharp, insistent colors of her clothes and even of her skin, her hair, were painful to her children's eyes. They had hated her. They had wished her dead. (167)

When she dies, Saul persuades his brothers not to attend her funeral. The land is sold and the house of Emory disappears forever; what remains, however, is not Poe's silent tarn, but an Amoco station.

What is intriguing about these two family houses is the carefully worked out chiastic connection between their inhabitants. Both Charlotte and Saul feel dissatisfied with their own lives and wish to cross over and live the other's. Charlotte, who resents her reclusive mother and fears a lifelong imprisonment, longs to be the daughter of the mercurial Alberta, and that wish is behind her marriage to Alberta's son Saul. She confronts the depth of this emotion when Alberta dies:

> When it came to matters of importance, I thought, I was not remotely a part of that family. Here I assumed I had broken into their circle, found myself some niche in the shelter of

114

Alberta's shadow, but it turned out the Emorys were as shut away as ever and Alberta had gone and died. Underneath I had always expected her back, I believe. I wanted her approval; she was so much braver, freer, stronger than I had turned out to be. There were a thousand things I had planned on holding up for her to pass judgment on. (156)

Just as Charlotte has wished she could switch mothers with Saul, so Saul succeeds in switching both mothers and houses with Charlotte. A wild young man, he discovers after he is engaged that he has a calling for the ministry. He moves into Charlotte's house and then over the next few years gathers all his brothers there as well, in the stable home he always wanted but that had been denied him by Alberta. When Charlotte's mother is dying of cancer, "She asked only for Saul. Wanted him to read to her from the big old family Bible; Psalms. . . . You would think this was his mother. First he'd had Alberta and now he had Mama, and here I was with nobody" (188).

The psychological name for the syndrome behind Saul and Charlotte's domestic crossover is *primitive idealization*. Clinical psychology has observed a tendency in children to focus their longing on an object outside the self and the family, to envision it as perfect, and to hope unreasonably that it will bring them transcendence. (The word *primitive* indicates that the process begins prior to the establishment of a mature demarcation between self and world, when narcissistic processes are still active.) Idealization is a subject that occurs in all Tyler's novels, but it holds a central position in those from *Earthly Possessions* through *Morgan's Passing* (in Morgan's obsession with Emily and Leon Meredith) and receives its most brilliant treatment in the utopian replacements for family that the Tull children concoct in *Dinner at the Homesick Restaurant*.

The most complete elucidation of the syndrome I have found is Heinz Kohut's *The Analysis of the Self.* Kohut classifies idealization as a narcissistic disorder, both because of the immaturity of the sufferer and because of the sufferer's tendency to focus on an object that is not truly autonomous from the self. For Kohut, the condition occurs when "the equilibrium of primary Narcissism is disturbed by the unavoidable shortcomings of maternal care, but the child replaces the previous perfection (a) by establishing a grandiose and exhibitionistic image of the self: *the grandiose self;* and (b) by giving over the previous perfection to an admired, omnipotent transitional self-object: *the idealized parent imago.*"[10] Kohut observes the possibility of the persistence of primitive idealization throughout adult life:

> If the child suffers the traumatic loss of the idealized object, however, or a traumatic disappointment in it, then optimal internalization does not take place. The child does not acquire the needed internal structure, his psyche remains fixated on an archaic self-object, and the personality will throughout life be dependent on certain objects in what seems to be an intense form of object hunger. The intensity of the search for and of the dependency on these objects is due to the fact that they are striven for as a substitute for the missing segment of the psychic structure.[11]

The narrative structure of *Earthly Possessions* grows like a crystal from the idea of primitive idealization, forming repeating patterns of intersecting lines, or a sort of narrative chiasm. The crisscrossing of the two narratives, between odd and even chapters, mirrors the characters' attempts to jump the tracks of their own fate and land in someone else's. As well as occurring *between* the two narratives, with Charlotte's swapping of Saul for Jake, house for car, immobility for flight, this crisscrossing also happens repeatedly *within* each of the narratives. I have mentioned Charlotte and Saul's idealizations of each other's homes. Charlotte marries Saul because she hopes he is

10. Heinz Kohut, *The Analysis of the Self: A Systematic Approach to the Psychoanalytic Treatment of Narcissistic Personality Disorders* (New York: International Universities Press, 1971), 25.

11. Ibid., 45.

shiftless like his mother; and he turns stolid and immobile. He marries Charlotte because she has never left her home; once they are married, she speaks daily of her plans to leave him, acting out her need for disencumbrance by throwing out all his mother's furniture. Crisscrossing also occurs within the narrative of flight, with Jake's visit to the idealized Oliver Jamison.

Perhaps the most delicious chiasm in the novel comes with Saul's "conversion." In the basement of the Holy Basis Church, Saul hears the singing voices of himself and his brothers when they were children and interprets it as a sign from God. Charlotte, who wants only to leave Clarion and her mother forever, says, "Well. I was so stunned I couldn't even take in air. I mean I just wasn't prepared for this, nothing that had happened up till now had given me the faintest inkling. I said, 'But . . . but, Saul . . .'" (95), and the reader can hear the whispered echo of Acts of the Apostles—"Why do you persecute me?" Charlotte concludes, "Although I didn't believe in God, I could almost change my mind now and imagine one, for who else would play such a joke on me? The only place more closed in than this house was a church. The only person odder than my mother was a hellfire preacher" (96). Saul is not "converted" in any palpable sense; he is not made new. He grows more leaden with every passing chapter. He simply succeeds in acting out the idealization of Charlotte's homebound life, in turn preventing her from taking up the shiftlessness of an Emory.

Parables of entrapment in the flesh pervade *Earthly Possessions*. Charlotte's mother wins back a degree of sympathy when, as she lies dying, she says, "How long am I going to be ruled by physical things? When do I get rid of this body?" (194). One of the fundamental observations of Tyler's fiction is that human beings are unique among living things in the tentativeness with which they accept embodiment and the destiny it dictates. When Charlotte, as an adolescent, discovered she was growing breasts, she tried to starve them off. Tyler's characters resent the fact that even an ordinary life is inalterable, as if the compensation for living unremarkably should be a multiplication of opportunities. Singleness of identity is a thing with which these characters feel unfairly burdened.

Their response is to weave fantasies of foundlinghood. Charlotte's mother was so startled when Charlotte was born that she developed a notion that the hospital had switched babies and this skinny, brown-haired child belonged to someone else. Charlotte comes to believe it. At age seven, as she sits on the "Beautiful Child" throne in the farm products tent of the county fair, she willingly allows herself to be kidnapped by a gaunt refugee woman who lives as a guest in a man's trailer and is entirely unencumbered, having walked away from everything, even her children, somewhere in Europe. When Charlotte is found and restored to her mother, she feels kidnapped. The life one idealizes is like the photographic negative of one's own, or like the upside-down people Charlotte sees in the viewfinder of her camera. When her mother is dying, Charlotte finds a photograph of a little girl in the drawer and assumes it is her mother's true child, the one the hospital had lost. When Charlotte has her first child, she refuses anesthesia in order to insure that no switches occur. When her daughter, Catherine, is older, she invents an imaginary friend, Selinda, with whom she switches identities. From then on, Selinda plays with her imaginary friend Catherine. Furthermore, Saul brings home an orphan from the church, and Charlotte names him Jiggs to enforce a casualness in her maternal feelings, in case someday she has to give him up. Jiggs does not encumber Charlotte: he is somebody else's earthly possession.

Inevitably, the title *Earthly Possessions* calls up a scriptural context. One thinks of Christ and the young rich man who cannot bring himself to sell all in order to get treasures in heaven (Matthew 19:20–22), or of Paul speaking to the Philippians on the enemies of Christ, "whose God is their belly, and whose glory is their shame, who mind earthly things" (Philippians 3:19). There is a conceptual chiasm here: Saul the preacher accumulates earthly things, and it is the nonbeliever Charlotte who goes to the bank to sell all she has and follow Jake. "A husband," Charlotte says, "is an encumbrance." "Possessions make me anxious" (41). Charlotte instinctively acts in ways that parody Christian imperatives. It is out of an inner compulsion, not through obedience, that she renounces the world and the flesh. Meanwhile, her husband speaks Christian imperatives and fills the house with two sets of furniture.

Thus the novel invites us to compare Charlotte to Saul in terms of the Christianity that he professes, and toward which she strives for a polite indifference. Saul Emory is neither a lily of the field nor a bird of the air. He persuades himself of his miraculous conversion because he needs a refuge. Charlotte is shocked at how quickly after their marriage he has settled her into a role and largely forgotten her. His repeated slogan is "I know you love me, Charlotte." But of his own love he does not speak. He is no better at forgiveness; when his brother Linus worries that Saul's heart is hardened against their mother, Charlotte says, "Oh, well, let him have one sin" (158). In a sense, Saul is Macon Leary seen from an objective distance: his Christianity is a compulsive system, a closing down of the psyche, which his brother Amos explains as a reaction to their mother's instability (interestingly, Macon Leary's mother is a precise repetition of Alberta). Saul's ministry shrinks as the book unfolds, and he finds himself mostly visiting deathbeds. Even his attempt to comfort Charlotte's dying mother eventually fails. She finds no satisfaction in the Psalms and banishes him. Then she invites Charlotte back and confronts her dying directly. Saul's ministry is ineffectual; it is ultimately circumscribed to the act of bringing people home, where it is Charlotte who takes care of them. By the time Charlotte leaves, Saul has introduced to the household all of his brothers, two boarders from the Holy Basis Church, the foundling Jiggs, and a dog named Earnest who loses control of his bladder when he cannot find Charlotte.

Charlotte cannot abide Christianity because it induces

spiritual claustrophobia in her. Having stayed home after high school to take care of her parents, and then having gotten permanently mired there by marrying Saul, she has to leave some windows open. She agrees to attend Holy Basis as a dutiful minister's wife, but she is physically incapable of focusing on Saul's sermons. She explains her attitude toward religion in a conversation with Jake:

> 'Is it my fault I'm not religious?' I never have been, not since I was seven and they gave me this book of children's Bible stories, this jealous God throwing tantrums, people having to sacrifice their children, everybody always in the wrong. I didn't like it. See, it's not that I don't *believe*. Sometimes I do, sometimes I don't, it depends on when you ask me. What the trouble is: I don't approve. I'd rather not be associated with it. It's against my principles. (182)

The God Charlotte describes resembles Tyler's fat ladies—he tyrannically imposes burdens through the infliction of guilt. Her mother's child, Charlotte inevitably became a person upon whom domestic burdens fall; while she rejects them in principle, she has become in fact the caretaker and servant in Saul's household. After her mother's death, Amos asks her to leave Saul and go away with him, and Charlotte refuses:

> "I'd assumed it was your mother," he said. "I assumed it was *duty*, that you'd leave in an instant if not for her. Turns out I was wrong. Here you are free to go, but then you always were, weren't you? You could have left any day of your life, but hung around waiting to be sprung. Passive. You're passive, Charlotte. You stay where you're put. . . .
> "Every year you've settled for less, tolerated more. You're the kind who thinks tolerance is a virtue." (205)

Charlotte's life had been a paradigm of unworldliness, passivity, and service. But these are instinctive traits, not responses to the Gospel's imperatives. When she gets on the road, her "Christian" attributes become more clearly

120

defined, and more problematic. Charlotte and Jake establish a secret-sharer relationship, a sexless spiritual affinity. Between the two of them, Tyler sketches a version of the soul's restlessness and its capacity for communion that religion as Saul practices it cannot quiet or comprehend.

Like the refugee woman whom Charlotte envisioned as her "true" mother, Jake is a kidnapper. It is unlikely, since her previous attempt to leave Saul failed, that Charlotte would have ever gotten away had Jake not taken her hostage. That fact qualifies the idea that flight is equal to freedom. Jake is an alternative husband, and ironically he is an idealization, a schematic antithesis, of Saul. First, Jake shares Charlotte's view of the material world: he travels light (he does not even carry a wallet), and he is a professional demolition derby driver. At twenty-three, he is like a loop in time; he is the man Charlotte should have married sixteen years before, a fantasy of starting over. He hungers for freedom, not money, and robbed the bank only to get the means to rescue Mindy from the unwed mother's home, so his child would not be "born in a prison." Prison is a place Jake cannot abide.

Thus his first affinity with Charlotte is their common claustrophobia. Jake has anxiety attacks in jail. He escaped just prior to the bank holdup because he felt closed in. Charlotte has repeated anxiety attacks in closed spaces—a bar, a ladies' room. She feels comfortable in only one such place, Jake's front seat, which becomes increasingly a domestic space on wheels as they head south, eating and sleeping in the car, picking up Mindy and her cat along the way. One of the funnier moments in their flight comes when Charlotte, who has inherited a little of her mother's agoraphobia, becomes panicky on the street near the Baltimore bus station and thinks of Jake with his gun as her "safe person." She begins to depend on him, a luxury denied her at home; when he stirs sugar into her coffee, she remembers: "I felt comforted. All I had to do was lift the cup, which was warm and heavy and solid. Everything else had been seen to. I was so well taken care of" (87).

Like Charlotte, Jake is subject to idealization. He thinks of the trip south as an opportunity to reestablish ties with his own ideal person, Oliver Jamison, an explosives specialist (and thus another anti-materialist) whom he admired in reform school. The authorities could lock Oliver up anywhere and he'd be indifferent; he would just read. Jake cannot accomplish this spiritual withdrawal, so he idealizes it. Also, Oliver explained to Jake that he was a "victim of impulse"—a phrase that Jake feels goes to the heart of himself—and he is grateful for Oliver's willingness to bear witness to his life. But when Jake finds Oliver in Perth, Florida, Oliver no longer blows up earthly possessions with dynamite; he has taken on a wife and child, made a home for his mother, and opened a restaurant.

It slowly dawns on Jake, with Charlotte's help, that he is traveling toward a similar fate with Mindy. At the same time, he explains to Charlotte that she has underestimated Saul, who does think she is a good woman. Hence Charlotte sees that her journey, too, is toward "home." Conspirators and mutual witnesses, Charlotte and Jake develop a telepathic capacity. It is clear that they will both end up with spouses with whom conversation is mostly pull and tug, complaint and miscomprehension. Mindy's only weapon against Jake is tears; Charlotte will return to a marriage that is perennially tense.

Thus, there is something uncommonly sweet in the perfect communication between the two doomed fugitives, Charlotte and Jake. Tyler's dialogue captures its magic. Here for instance, are Jake and Charlotte looking at a skiing poster in the window of a travel agency:

"You ever skied?"

"Not even once," I said. "I always wanted to, though."

"You reckon it's dangerous?"

"Well, a little, maybe."

"I got a feeling I'd be good at it," he told me. "I know that sounds conceited."

"Maybe we should have gone north instead of south," I said.

"Someplace cold."
"Someplace with clear, cold air."
"Well," Jake said, sighing.
"Well." (144)

Jake understands the affinity between himself and Charlotte; when she decides to go home, he acknowledges his need for her:

"Charlotte, but . . . see, I can't quite manage without you just yet. Understand? I've got this pregnant woman on my hands, got all these . . . Charlotte, it ain't so bad if you're *with* us, you see. You act like you take it all in stride, like this is the way life really does tend to turn out. You mostly wear this little smile. I mean, we know each other Charlotte. Don't we?" (218–19)

Jake's car, like Jeremy's boardinghouse or Ezra's restaurant, is a home away from home—it magnifies the paradoxes of the issue it models, which in this book is marriage. Jake and Charlotte bear each other witness. They do not intrude on each other in the inevitable way of real spouses. Therefore, their circumstances parody Christian marriage: they achieve a kind of happiness while Jake holds Charlotte hostage at gunpoint, while Charlotte weighs Jake down, impedes his escape. Their friendship briefly transcends the circumstantial world toward which both must travel—the endless accommodations of domestic life that wear away the magic of mutuality. Jake explains the soul's longing for flight:

"The trouble is," said Jake, "when people are thinking ill of you you just have this urge to get out, you know? You say, now if I could just gather myself together again. If I could just start my life over somehow."
"That's true," I said.
"I really believe," he told me, "that any time you see someone running, it's their old, faulty self they're running from. Or other people's *notion* of their faulty self." (175)

For Tyler, there is sufficiency in this explanation. Self-hood has no unimposed core. Guilt and the soul are parts of an ideology of entrapment. Flight, or fantasy, despite its ultimate futility, is a legitimate means of gaining perspective. It may provide the only opportunity to set down the truth about "home." Tyler equates it with Charlotte's photography studio, where she strews costumes and props that her customers are invited to pick up and pose with. On the novel's last page, Charlotte reverts to taking those pictures: "And I still wheel my camera around, recording upside-down people in unexpected costumes. But I've come to believe that their borrowed medals may tell more truths than they hide" (221–22). As she had observed earlier, "People are only reflections in other people's eyes, it turns out" (157). In a limited but clarifying sense, one can speak of Tyler's theology. It stops short of a doctrine; it possesses no force of law. It has no concept of sin and no eschatology. But it acknowledges as valid the Christian feeling of being out of place in the world, the spirit's restlessness.

Admittedly, it is a circular argument to try to discover the roots of Charlotte's character in Tyler's own Quaker upbringing. Suffice it to say that common threads are visible. Charlotte is a character who refuses to conform to external molds, to adhere to doctrines. She listens to her own interior promptings. She is quietistic and passive. Both at home and with Jake, she sustains people, she provides a sense of community. In her photography and in her life, she acts as a witness; she allows others to imagine themselves in untarnished form and generously sees that there is truth in such imagining.

VII *DINNER AT THE HOMESICK RESTAURANT*

In *Dinner at the Homesick Restaurant,* Anne Tyler quarrels with Tolstoy's famous dictum. Unhappy families may not be alike in specifics, she argues, but there are two underlying principles they do hold in common. First, members of an unhappy family onerously interpret the past, finding in it an explanation for present imperfections. Second, their efforts to wrestle free from the past are tainted with narcissism;[1] they conduct a futile search in the outside world for an "idealized" self. Like Duncan Peck, they think they are reaching out toward the new and the other, but they are mostly stuck inverting the old and the same. Like Kafka's burrowing animal, they supposedly dig toward freedom but only succeed in building more complex labyrinths of interiority.[2] A book of memory and dreaming, *Dinner at the Homesick Restaurant* asserts the humanity, not just the pathology, of these two principles—obsession with the past and idealization. The novel demonstrates, in subdued comic form, how families often heal their members, but always wound them first.

Pearl Cody, after a narrow brush with old-maidhood, married Beck Tull, a salesman for the Tanner Corporation whose greatest need is to please people. After the births of three children, Cody, Ezra, and Jenny, Beck informed

1. Anne Jones uses the term to classify certain characters in Tyler's fiction. It is probably more accurate to think of narcissism as a universal stage of development, the vestiges of which are more pronounced in some adult characters than in others. See "Home at Last and Homesick Again," 5.

2. On the second page of the novel, Pearl Tull anxiously reconstructs the defensive paradoxes of Kafka's Burrow when she discovers she needs "extra" children.

125

Pearl one Sunday night in 1944 that he did not want to be married, and he left the family forever.

We learn later that an event that occurred only a few months beforehand crystallized Beck's sense of his inability to live up to Pearl's high expectations. Beck had taken the children on an outing to play with a new archery set. Cody aimed an arrow at Ezra, who jumped on him to prevent the shot. In the tussle, the arrow wounded Pearl in the shoulder. At the hospital, she received penicillin and almost died. Beck cannot bear the moral murkiness of such situations. He moves on to a life in which ambiguous guilt cannot dim his boyishly chipper self-image. But his departure has consequences.

Pearl, through an anxious, compulsive effort, punctuated by fits of maternal rage, manages to raise the children alone. The determinative myths of selfhood that the children take away from their troubled upbringing, the idealizations they inspire, and Cody's final liberation from the process are the subject of the novel.

In angry flight from his mother, Cody Tull, the oldest child, and the one most damaged by the failure of his parents' marriage, becomes an aggressive, quarrelsome efficiency expert. His itinerant life keeps him from Baltimore, but he ironically repeats the joyless orderliness he perceived in his mother's bureau drawers. His brother Ezra creates and manages a restaurant that corrects the excessive closeness of his family with an atmosphere that consoles the customer while making no demands. Jenny, the youngest, becomes a pediatrician, a professional mother who can evade stifling emotional obligations.

Cody's efficiency, Ezra's restaurant, and Jenny's pediatrics are significant because they represent lifelong programs through which these characters attempt to get free of the selves their family formed for them. They are parables of primitive idealization, the syndrome that characterized Saul and Charlotte in *Earthly Possessions*, the pressing of one's nose against the windows of other people's "happy" homes. The Tull children dream of rescuers who will come and take them away from their fairy-tale witch of a mother. Jenny leaps into a marriage with Harley Baines because he is a paragon of control—a person who will never fly into the kind of rage she fears in Pearl. Cody wildly idealizes Ruth Spivey, calling her "perfect." He steals her from Ezra because she signifies the goodness that Cody envies in his brother. Ezra idealizes Mrs. Scarlatti, the mother who never invades his emotional privacy. In his guilt at her death, he never realizes that his Homesick Restaurant began as a monument to his ideal relationship with her.

Children of normal capacities find people to idealize—the charming couple who will come and save them from the tacky parental impostors with whom they live. The Tull children are prodigies of idealization. In their need to heal a childhood wound, they build emotional utopias, spatial and conceptual extensions of the primitive urge toward idealization: Cody's unoccupied farmhouse where his phantom family lives in perfect bliss, Ezra's restaurant without walls, Jenny's career and impossibly casual marriage. True to Tyler's own imaginative tendencies, they revert less naturally to hero worship than to architecture, or to inventory.

Jenny's ill-adjusted adolescent stepson, Slevin, occasions a small interlude in the novel on this form of primitive idealization. (So, by the way, do all the people Cody's son, Luke, meets when he hitchhikes north in chapter 8.) Slevin's actual mother has abandoned him; on a visit to Pearl's house with Jenny, he finds a vacuum cleaner just like the one his mother owned. The wave of nostalgia is so powerful that Slevin steals the vacuum, a symbol of the ideally domestic mother that the world will not provide. In her bemused conversation with Slevin's priest, Jenny reveals her clinical as well as her personal familiarity with the pathology.[3] Her vision of Slevin's idealizing has the profuseness of a Luis Buñuel film:

3. Remember that Tyler's husband, Tagi Modarressi, is a pediatric psychiatrist.

127

"What's next, I wonder," Jenny said. She mused for a moment. "Picture it! Grand pianos. Kitchen sinks. Why, we'll have his mother's whole household," she said, "her photo albums and her grade school year-books, her college roommate asleep on our bed and her high school boyfriends in our living room." She pictured a row of dressed-up boys from the fifties, their hair slicked down wetly, their shirts ironed crisply, perched on her couch like mannequins with heart-shaped boxes of chocolates on their knees.[4]

Pearl is the one who carries the germ of this particular illness. An orphan herself, Pearl was driven to marry Beck by her own susceptibility to an idealizing sense of public propriety. She tried to match an ideal picture of a young lady's life. She dreaded being an old maid, and later she felt the same dread toward childlessness. Her sense of social embarrassment is acute; after Beck leaves, she never admits the fact of his betrayal to her relatives back home, her neighbors, or even her children. Instead, she employs her practical skills to make the home airtight and efficient, her manipulative skills to bind her children to her. Yet she is nagged by the sense that her own family has failed to meet the external standard that imprisons her imagination. At one point, late in life, she indulges in the signal act of idealization—imagining the lives of other, "happy" families:

Often, like a child peering over the fence at somebody else's party, she gazes wistfully at other families and wonders what their secret is. They seem so close. Is it that they're more religious? Or stricter, or more lenient? Could it be the fact that they participate in sports? Read books together? Have some common hobby? Recently, she overheard a neighbor woman discussing her plans for Independence Day: her family was having a picnic. Every member—child or grownup—was

4. *Dinner at the Homesick Restaurant* (New York: Berkeley Books, 1983), 28–29. Hereafter cited parenthetically in the text by page number.

cooking his or her specialty. Those who were too little to cook were in charge of the paper plates.

Pearl felt such a wave of longing that her knees went weak. (189)

Of all the Tulls, Cody suffers the worst divisions in consequence of his idealizing. A perspicacious child (and a snoopy one), Cody saw his mother's disappointment in a certain setting of her jaw. Inadvertently, Pearl taught Cody to be embarrassed at his hapless father's loud suits, worn-through rayon socks, and the curled-up shoes he stepped into without first untying the laces. In consequence, Cody as an adult is torn between a bold but jejune pragmatism and a secret, half-acknowledged dream of emotional fulfillment. Like Pearl, he conceives of unhappiness as a problem to be solved—a problem of mathematics, money, and managing.

Ezra is not so divided. He becomes an affectionate, unconflicted man who reconstructs his unhappy family in the form of a supreme fiction. Pearl as a mother was too intrusive, too smothering, and she drove the other children to greater and greater distances. In gentle but stubborn reaction to his past, Ezra opens a restaurant that is not a home but as a home might be—a consoling place, where the perfect balance of emotional closeness and distance is attained, where a meal is a source of comfort, not an occasion for bitterness, breakup, and lonely retreat. Ezra's restaurant is an extension of his own nurturing soul. His mother could not feed; she poured canned peas over the children's heads. Ezra dedicates his adult life to the sacramental aspect of dinner, a melting away of differences in a higher commonality.

Ezra's emotional utopia is socialistic, an economic antithesis to Cody's capitalist drive. The restaurant's motto might well be "From each according to his ability, to each according to his need." He prescribes meals for his customers, and he charges them what he thinks they can afford. While Cody dreams of a stable and isolated nuclear family, Ezra's staff is a rainbow coalition and his menu—which changes nightly—is composed of ethnic dishes from several continents.

Jenny attempts to establish a similar emotional distance in her own life by, first, reconstructing motherhood as pediatrics and, second, marrying a man with too many children. After her nervous breakdown, in which—exhausted and husbandless—she abuses her own child, she trains herself to go through life "on a slant." With the children of her third husband, she establishes insouciance as her step-maternal tone, insuring that she will never again turn into Pearl.

Jenny suffers the purest and most poignant attack of idealization in the book. Ezra goes off to boot camp—it is 1952—and asks Jenny to visit his lunky friend Josiah Payson, whom everyone in school had shunned as mentally deranged. She accepts an invitation to dinner at Josiah's:

> Supper was spaghetti and a salad, with chocolate cake for dessert. Jenny ate sparingly, planning to eat again when she got home so her mother wouldn't guess; but Josiah had several helpings of everything. Mrs. Payson kept refilling his plate. "To look at him," she said, "you'd never know he eats so much, would you? Skinny as a fence post. I reckon he's still a growing boy." She laughed, and Josiah grinned bashfully with his eyes cast down—a skeletal, stooped, hunkering man. Jenny had never thought about the fact that Josiah was somebody's son, some woman's greatest treasure. His stubby black lashes were lowered; his prickly head was bent over his plate. He was certain of being loved, here if no place else. She looked away. (78–79)

When Jenny's mother finds Jenny and Josiah on her front step that night, she slaps Jenny and insults Josiah bitterly. But Josiah is not that easily banished from memory. When Jenny sees him again, after his mother has died, she realizes something about herself:

> "I've thought of you often," Jenny said.
> She didn't mean it, at first. But then she understood,

with a rush to her head that was something like illness, that she spoke the truth: she had been thinking of him all these years without knowing it. It seemed he had never once left her mind. Even Harley, she saw, was just a reverse kind of Josiah, a Josiah turned inside out: equally alien, black-and-white, incomprehensible to anyone but Jenny. (106-7)

Josiah's persistence in Jenny's mind is the consequence of a powerful moment of idealization. Josiah had mistaken Jenny's stunned interest in his home for love. He kissed her, and Jenny "saw things suddenly from his viewpoint: their gentle little 'romance' (was what he must call it), as seamless as the Widow Payson's fairy tale existence. She longed for it; she wished it were true. She ached, with something like nostalgia, for a contented life with his mother in her snug house, for an innocent, protective marriage" (79-80).

This is the curious thing about the Tulls: every one of them is susceptible to dizzying attacks of nostalgia, but for a life other than their own. A leaping off the tracks of memory, this variation on nostalgia brings up the subject of the past, its power to shape ideal imaginings, and the all-important role of time in the novel. Most readers of Tyler agree that *Dinner at the Homesick Restaurant* represents a significant heightening of her imaginative powers over previous novels, and it is very likely the palpable presence of time, and the complex narrative form she employs to establish it, that gives her ninth published novel the uncanny rightness of its temporal illusionism.

The narrative structure of the novel radically rearranges the chronology of its events. There are ten chapters. Each is located in the memory of a single character (except chapter 8, "This Really Happened," which is shared by Cody and his son, Luke). Most establish a dramatic present, a "meditating time," and then loop backward in memory to recall past events in "meditated time." Doris Betts, in an article entitled "The Fiction of Anne Tyler," reported learning from the author's mother that each of these chapters was designed to stand alone as a short story.[5] Rhetorically, each chapter begins by introducing the characters anew, as if nothing had come before. This radical discreteness of the chapters breaks up any linear, cause-and-effect exposition, inhibiting any sense of determinism. For instance, versions of the archery scene recur in four chapters, each remembered by a different character, with a different emotional resonance, a contradictory attributing of blame, so that we never conclude who was responsible for wounding Pearl, or whether the archery scene was a cause or merely an exemplum of the family's trouble. The autonomy of the chapters also underscores the isolation of each member of the family, as he or she constructs a map of memory that never matches—and sometimes fails to resemble—anyone else's. In short, the novel's narrative design imitates the way a family remembers its past.

The book opens in Pearl's mind in free drift as she lies on her deathbed in 1979. Pearl recalls her girlhood, her marriage to Beck, the arrival of their children, and his departure. Chapter 1 narrates her perusal, with Ezra's help, of her diaries. Seven chapters intervene, and then chapter 9, "Apple Apple," continues the diary reading, until Pearl reaches the epiphanic moment in which she was perfectly happy, in the spring of 1910. She dies shortly after that.

Those intervening seven chapters provide the children's memories and develop their utopian life projects. Chapter 2 provides parables from the 1940s of Cody's ambivalence toward his "lucky" brother Ezra, "the favorite." Chapter 3 comprises three temporal settings—1952, 1957, and 1958. It tells of Jenny's escape from home to college and marriage, her *Märchen*-like discovery of Josiah Payson, and her nervous breakdown. Chapter 4, set in 1955, is the story of Ezra, the restaurant, and his "extra" mother, Mrs.

5. "The Fiction of Anne Tyler," 36. Only chapter 5, "The Country Cook," was ever published separately as a short story, in *Harper's* 264 (March 1982): 54–62.

Scarlatti. Chapter 5 tells the story of Cody's theft of Ezra's girlfriend Ruth, the "Country Cook," in 1960.

Chapter 6, "Beaches on the Moon," is an *entr'acte,* reminiscent of the "Time Passes" section of Virginia Woolf's *To the Lighthouse.* Its meditating times are numerous, even composite—it tells of three visits a year for about seven years to clean Cody's farmhouse. A prose elegy, it moves backward over meditated times of unfulfillment—Cody's enforced itinerancy; Ezra's lonely routines. Its function is not so much to read more anecdotes into the record as it is to show the inexorability of time's passing, the absence of second chances. Chapter 7, "Dr. Tull Is Not a Toy," tells about Jenny as a pediatrician in 1973, Jenny's life "on a slant," and her troubled stepson, Slevin. Chapter 8, "This Really Happened," begins in Cody's point of view, after his near-fatal accident in the factory in 1975; then, after Cody accuses Ruth of conceiving their son, Luke, with Ezra, it shifts to Luke's perspective as he hitchhikes to Baltimore to visit his uncle at the Homesick Restaurant. The chapter is a Chaucerian account of Route 95; its purpose is to demonstrate that the Tulls' troubles are virtually everybody's, as Luke hitches a series of rides with vivid, slightly crazed, absolutely credible middle Americans searching the freeway for an exit from their pain. Chapter 9 completes Pearl's diary inquiry, and chapter 10 delineates her funeral, Beck's appearance there, and the epiphanic release of Cody.

Tyler has meditated on the weighty influence of time in all her novels, and in several she has pondered the magical way a photograph can freeze a moment, so that decades later its subject can gaze at it and feel the pull of ties to a previous self, or check it for change like a barometer. In *Dinner at the Homesick Restaurant,* she goes a step farther, undertaking an inquiry into philosophic conceptions of time, grounding the novel's narrative form in the time theories of the ancient Greeks. The frozen moment—important to the plots and characters of earlier novels—becomes the technical building block, the atomic particle, of this one.

The pre-Socratic philosophers shifted between two conceptualizations of time. The first was that it was a fluid entity, divisible into infinitely smaller segments of duration. The second was that it was cinematographic, a series of indivisible units, irreducible freeze-frames. The Pythagoreans developed a theory of number that allowed them to explain motion by shifting inconsistently between these two definitions. Zeno of Elea devised four arguments in order to trap the Pythagoreans by demonstrating that their explanation of motion was not compatible with either the fluid or the cinematographic definition of time, if they would consistently adhere to one or the other.

In "the Arrow," Zeno's third paradox, he cited the Pythagorean definition of an object at rest as "occupying a space equal to its own dimensions." Starting from the premise of the "cinematographic" theory, he postulated an arrow in flight; at any point in the arrow's trajectory, it could be said to occupy a space equal to its own dimensions at that indivisible moment of time. It is also possible to imagine the arrow subsequently in an adjacent frame; but if the frames are indeed irreducible, it is never possible to imagine the arrow moving between them. Hence, by the Pythagorean definition, the arrow is "at rest" at each moment, and therefore there is no time in which the arrow moves, so the cinematographic theory of time disallows the possibility of motion.[6]

Dinner at The Homesick Restaurant constructs time as a series of cinematographic frames, "atomic nows."[7] The novel provides emotionally significant durations of time and measures them in metaphorical increments. For example, there is the darkening of Cody's dream house that

6. For a concise account, see G. S. Kirk and J. E. Raven, *The Pre-Socratic Philosophers* (Cambridge: Cambridge University Press, 1957), 291–97. Also, H. D. P. Lee, *Zeno of Elea* (Cambridge: Cambridge University Press, 1936), 78–83.

7. Lee, *Zeno of Elea*, 78.

Pearl perceives as she watches Ezra sequentially close off the window mullions with cardboard. She measures the passage of time, and the deepening of Cody's home-sickness, by the incremental darkening of the house:

Ezra tapes squares of cardboard to the broken windowpanes. He works steadily, doggedly. She looks up once and sees how the sweat has made an eagle-shaped stain across his back. There are other cardboard squares on other panes, broken earlier. In a few more seasons, it occurs to her, they'll be working in the dark. It's as if they're sealing themselves in, windowpane by windowpane. (173).

This incrementation occurs repeatedly. Jenny leaves Harley behind for a visit home to think. As Jenny rides the train into the Baltimore station, Tyler pauses to perform a demonstration of Pythagorean incremental motion: "She rubbed a clean spot on the window and stared out at acres of railroad track, then at the first metal posts flying by, then at slower posts, better defined, and a dark flight of stairs" (99–100). Or consider the haunting quality that a conception of time as a series of frames can evoke. One weekend during the epoch of his obsession with Ruth, Cody does not go to Baltimore, but then he dreams of her:

She was waiting for a train that he was traveling on. He saw her on the platform, peering into the windows of each passenger car as it slid by. He was so eager to reach her, to watch her expression ease when she caught sight of him, that he called her name aloud and woke himself up. He heard it echoing in the dark—not her name after all, but some mean-ingless sleep sound. For hours after that he tried to burrow back inside the dream, but he had lost it. (158–59)

Each of these instances imagines time as slowing incre-mentally toward an irreducible moment, just as it does in the seconds before a photograph is taken in *The Tin Can Tree*. Jenny comes very close to a full stop when she is seized by anxiety as she returns to the empty Baltimore house after her brothers are gone: "In the afternoons when she came home from school, her mother would still be at work, and Jenny would open the door and hesitantly step inside. Sometimes it seemed there was a startled motion, or a stopping of motion, somewhere deep in the house just as she crossed the threshold. She'd pause then, heart thumping, alert as a deer, but it never turned out to be anything real" (69).

This use of an incremental series of still moments structures the entirety of Chapter 6, "Beaches on the Moon," the composite account of Pearl's visits to Cody's farmhouse, a narrative that imitates the action of flipping through a tablet of paper on which a figure has been drawn in a sequence of positions, to produce the illusion of motion.[8] Tyler seems increasingly to enjoy the metaphysical implications of her art, the ontological ironies of representation; and in this novel there is the hint of nascent Nabokovian interests.[9]

In *Dinner at the Homesick Restaurant,* time moves in loops as well as straight lines. Exhausted from thirty-six-hour call periods at the hospital and the work of raising Becky alone, Jenny collapses. Pearl comes to nurse her back to health and brings along a copy of *The Little House* to read to Becky:

Jenny had forgotten about *The Little House.* Why, she had loved that book! She'd requested it every evening, she remembered now. She'd sat on that homely old sofa and listened while her mother, with endless patience, read it three times, four times, five . . . Now Becky said, "Read it again," and Pearl returned to page one, and Jenny listened just as closely as Becky did. (215)

8. Zeno concluded that all motion was illusory: he accepted the evidence of logic over that of the senses.

9. Tyler plays one intertextual game. When Cody visits Ruth (pp. 149–65), he steps into Jeremy Pauling's boardinghouse from *Celestial Navigation.* Jeremy is there, hiding behind the refrigerator door. The reason Mrs. Pauling is fixated on pain during Cody's visit is that this is the spring of 1960; she will die of heart failure the following fall, and she is undoubtedly suffering from *angina,* perhaps the result of finding herself in the wrong novel.

136

This is a new experience to Jenny—nostalgia for her own past, which can be reopened, like *The Little House*. Listening to her mother read, Jenny unfolds a memory in which Pearl was patient, an opposing version of the past, triggered by a repetition. Tyler has written for the children's section of the *New York Times Book Review* of *The Little House*'s importance for her own childhood. She testifies to its power in forming her own sense of time, and she describes the power of a childhood book to summon the past and to teach fundamental philosophic concepts. Here is her summative paragraph:

> This brings me to what I see now as the real point of "The Little House." I believe the book spoke to me about something I hadn't yet consciously considered: the passage of time. And it introduced me to the feeling of nostalgia—the realization of the losses that the passage of time can bring. If the concept of a nostalgic 4-year-old strikes you as laughable, well, think about why that should be. Isn't it because children begin as creatures of the moment? And doesn't growing up mean the dawning knowledge that all moments are joined, each moment linked inexorably to the one that follows?[10]

In the novel, Jenny derives a degree of peace from the knowledge that she is linked to mother and daughter by this chain of irreducible—but repeatable—moments. It is through them that she frees herself from fear.

Jenny introduces the ambiguous power of time's circularity. Brutalizing Becky, she abhors the seemingly deterministic repetition of her mother in herself. Hearing *The Little House*, she experiences a loop in time that announces freedom instead of fate. But it is her brothers who schematize the novel on this issue of time. From the moment in which Cody aimed the bow at Ezra, Ezra jumped Cody, and the arrow began its trajectory toward Pearl, the two began to develop in antithetical directions. As adults, it is their opposed thinking about time that defines them. Cody has embraced the Greek idea of time

10. "Why I still Treasure 'The Little House.'"

termed *Chronos*—"the fundamental conception of time as measure, the quantity of duration, the length of periodicity, the age of an object or artifact, and the rate of acceleration as applied to the movement of identifiable bodies."[11] *Chronos* is objective, mechanical, clock time. Ezra, on the other hand, adheres to the concept of *Kairos*—time defined as "opportunity," or "occasion"—the single nodal moment toward and from which *Chronos* moves. "The other term—*Kairos*—points to a *qualitative* character of time, to the special position an event or action occupies in a series, to a season when something appropriately happens that cannot happen at 'any' time, but only at 'that time', to a time that marks an opportunity that may not recur."[12] Cody lives across the long series of moments; Ezra strives to create, enter, and occupy but one moment. Cody becomes an efficiency expert, whose occupation is to design sequences of motions across a duration: "*Joining object K to object L: right-hand transport unloaded, search, grasp, transport loaded . . . Unavoidable delays: 3. Avoidable delays: 9*" (136–37). Ezra opens a restaurant dedicated to one goal: seeing his family finish a dinner. If they were ever to succeed, it would be tantamount to a sacrament.

Tyler brilliantly and subtly embeds these concepts of time into her characters. Here is Cody, showing his mother the new car he just bought "on time": "I'm getting rich I tell you. Five years from now I can walk into an auto dealer, any dealer—Cadillac—and slap cold cash on the counter and say, 'I'll take three. Or on second thought, make that four'" (92). Time for Cody is a calculation of rates, a perception of trends. For Ezra, on the other hand, it is precisely an occasion, an opportunity, as is exemplified by a vignette in the hospital, when Mrs. Scarlatti is ill. Ezra comes across a little girl from a foreign family,

11. John E. Smith, "Time, Times, and the 'Right Time': *Chronos* and *Kairos*," *The Monist* 53 (January 1969): 1–13. This dichotomy was central to the theology of Paul Tillich. See also Mircea Eliade, *Cosmos and History: The Myth of Eternal Return* (New York: Harper Torchbooks, 1954).

12. Smith, "Time, Times," 1.

sleeping on a chair with metal arms. He wants to put his coat beneath her head but hesitates for fear of waking her. Then a woman comes out and makes her comfortable, and the child does not wake up: "So after all Ezra could have put his coat beneath her head. He had missed *an opportunity.* It was like missing a train—or something more important, something that would never come again. There was no explanation for the grief that suddenly filled him" (121, italics mine).

Tyler does not accord a clear moral superiority to Ezra over Cody. According to the terms established in her essay on *The Little House,* it is the child who lives in the moment, the adult who strings moments together. Cody, the adult, is effectual; his money and managerial skills provide real help to his family. There is arrested development behind Ezra's goodness; Pearl sees his unwillingness to fight for Ruth as masochism. On the other hand, Cody is not devoid of emotional limitations either. In the car with Luke, he explains his love of *Chronos*:

And when he started speaking again, it was on a whole different subject: time. How time was underestimated. How time was so important and all. Luke felt relieved. He listened comfortably, lulled by his father's words. "Everything," his father said, "comes down to time in the end—to the passing of time, to changing. Ever thought of that? Anything that makes you happy or sad, isn't it all based on minutes going by? Isn't happiness expecting something time is going to bring you? Isn't sadness wishing time back again? Even *big* things—even mourning a death: aren't you really wishing to have the time back when the person was alive? Or photos—ever notice old photographs? How wistful they make you feel? (262)

The flaw in Cody's conception, when applied to emotional life, is that it is premised on the unpossessability of the moment—his experience is made up entirely of memories and anticipations, with no possibility of a joyous entry into the "atomic now." Ezra's ease of access to that "now" is the source of Cody's envy: it is not Ezra's "luck" or his appeal to women, it is his maddening ability to remain blind to the segmenting of moments, to slip inside any single one and take a nap with his cat Alicia. For adherence to *Chronos* leads to another Greek concept, this one formulated by Woody Allen in the monologue sequence of *Annie Hall*. A woman Cody went out with once accused him of *anhedonia*:

> Watching him dissect his fish but then fail to eat it, noticing how he refused dessert and then benignly, tolerantly waited for her to finish a giant chocolate mousse, she had accused him of . . . what had she called it? Lack of enjoyment. Lack of ability to enjoy himself. He hadn't understood, back then, how she could draw so many implications from a single meal. (164)

Shortly after his accident, Cody talks to Luke about time and confesses that his deepest longing is to escape time, that all his efforts to manage it are a kind of compromise because his mysticism is untenable:

> "Time is my obsession: not to waste it, not to lose it. It's like . . . I don't know, an object, to me; something you can almost take hold of. If I could just collect enough of it in one clump, I always think. If I could pass it back and forth and sideways, you know? If only Einstein were right and time were a kind of river you could choose to step into at any place along the shore."
>
> He clicked his pen point in and out, frowning into space. "If they had a time machine, I'd go on it," he said. "It wouldn't much matter to me where. Past or future: just out of my time. Just someplace else."
>
> Luke felt a pang. "But then you wouldn't know *me*," he said.
>
> "Hmm?"
>
> "Sure he would," Ruth said briskly. She was opening the latches of Cody's briefcase. "He'd take you with him. Only mind," she told Cody, "if Luke goes too you've got to bring penicillin, and his hay fever pills, and fluoride toothpaste, you hear?"

140

Cody laughed, but he didn't say one way or another about taking Luke along. (228–29)

Chronological time has provided the clothesline on which Cody has hung instances of his family's injuries to himself. Perhaps his longing to transcend time stems from the burden he has made of it. Cody has become a historian, a chronicler of injuries, a gatherer of instances. Jenny neatly explains Cody's obsession with the past to Ezra, when Ezra innocently suggests that they send Cody some old family snapshots. She says that he is like the Lawsons, who moved to Baltimore and decided it was bad luck. Every unlucky thing that happened in the family was explained with the phrase, "Well, that's Baltimore."

"Well, now, I'm trying to follow you, here," Ezra said.
"It's whether you add up the list or not," Jenny said. "I mean, if you catalogue grudges, anything looks bad. And Cody certainly catalogues; he's running his life with his catalogues. But after all, I told him, we made it, didn't we? We did grow up. Why, the three of us turned out fine, just fine!" (204)

Chapter 8, in which Cody madly determines that Luke is Ezra's son, is entitled "This Really Happened." Of course, it did not, and that is the irony. But it is also revealing that Cody's paranoid view of his childhood always rests on objective events, things that "really happened," while he remains blind to his own subjective, distorting role in the chronicling of them. He tells Luke the story of the Christmas when he saved money for his mother to take a bus trip to visit her friend Emmaline. His mother refused the gift because it would have taken her away from home on Ezra's birthday, "proof" that Ezra was her favorite. What Cody cannot see is that he bought the ticket *in order* to arrive dramatically at this foregone conclusion. Luke listens to the story, sees it squarely, and defends Pearl. Cody gets furious, all over again.

141

Tyler wonderfully establishes the contrast between Cody's *Chronos* and Ezra's *Kairos,* always with a playful relativism, so that it can be viewed from either side. For instance, Cody thinks about Ezra and his repeated attempts at a family dinner:

Hadn't Ezra noticed (Cody wondered) that the family as a whole had never yet finished one of his dinners? That they'd fight and stamp off halfway through, or sometimes not even manage to get seated in the first place? Well, of course he must have *noticed,* but was it clear to him as a pattern, a theme? No, perhaps he viewed each dinner as a unit in itself, unconnected to the others. Maybe he never linked them in his mind.

Assuming he was a total idiot. (157)

From a practical point of view, there is something foolish about Ezra and his fixatedness inside the single unit of time, his inability to count instances. On the other hand, for those who understand it—and Cody will learn to—the Homesick Restaurant *is* the time machine Cody longs for. The most aching nostalgia is not for home but for home idealized, and the triumph of Ezra's lonely life has been the construction of such a place. The key to it, he knows, lies in never crowding people—the secret is reticence. When Jenny comes home without Harley, Pearl cajoles Ezra into interrogating her. He wisely fails, and then explains to his mother:

"I'm worried I don't know how to get in touch with people," Ezra said.

"Hmm?"

"I'm worried if I come too close, they'll say I'm overstepping. They'll say I'm pushy, or . . . emotional, you know. But if I back off, they might think I don't care. I really, honestly believe I missed some rule that everyone else takes for granted; I must have been absent from school that day. There's this narrow little dividing line I somehow never located."

>   "Nonsense; I don't know what you're talking about,"
> said his mother, and then she held up an egg.[13] (127)

The "narrow little dividing line" is another incremental image. There are lines between moments, lines between people. Both are shifting and hard to locate. Ezra instinctively studies their nature, respects them. His restaurant is the place where *Kairos,* the significant moment, can be manifest, where the individual human being will be nurtured but never intruded upon. Cody is right; the single unit is Ezra's realm, all that he sees.

The most significant quality of Ezra's view of time is that it—like the reading of *The Little House* that heals Jenny—is circular. Ezra does not really age, internally. Each day is much the same as the last, providing its opportunities to feed. For Ezra, the chronology of the novel is a cycle of holidays. He hopes with almost indefatigable optimism that the next will bring the family together for a completed meal.[14]

Ezra's denial of history, his view of time as a repeated sequence of potentially sacred moments, complements Cody's profanely historical vision. What Cody's emotional self seems ready to acknowledge is that his catalog of grievances begs for redress, or cancellation. It is Pearl's death, and her final gesture toward the healing of the family, that topples him into the atomic moment. Pearl asks Ezra to invite Beck to her funeral. Beck meets Cody and tells him he is proud of him—a "time-study" man. He disarms Cody, who wonders, now that the purpose of

13. For an interesting argument that this moment and others like it in Tyler have their origins in Eudora Welty, see Mary F. Robertson, "Anne Tyler: Medusa Points and Contact Points," in *Contemporary Women Writers: Narrative Strategies,* edited by Catherine Rainwater and William J. Scheik, 119–52. I am indebted to Elaine Gardiner and Catherine Rainwater for the invaluable bibliography of Tyler's work that accompanies Robertson's essay, and which rests in turn on the pioneering efforts of Stella Nesanovich.

14. Thanksgiving is the most frequently mentioned holiday in the book, although it dramatizes only one Thanksgiving dinner, a disaster. Christmas comes in second. Easter is third.

thirty years of workaholism is served, what will take him to the office on Monday. But then Beck's facile vision of the Tulls restores Cody's righteous anger, and he and Ezra, at last, debate their time philosophies, seeing them as ways of accounting for Pearl:

>"You think we're a family," Cody said, turning back. "You think we're some jolly, situation-comedy family when we're in particles, torn apart, torn all over the place, and our mother was a witch."
>
>"Oh Cody," Ezra said.
>
>"A raving, shrieking, unpredictable witch," Cody told Beck. "She slammed us against the wall and called us scum and vipers, said she wished us dead, shook us till our teeth rattled, screamed in our faces." . . .
>
>"It wasn't like that," Ezra said finally.
>
>"You're going to deny it?" Cody asked him.
>
>"No, but she wasn't always angry. Really she was angry very seldom, only a few times, widely spaced, that happened to stick in your mind."
>
>Cody felt drained. He looked at his dinner and found pink-centered lamb and bright vegetables—a perfect arrangement of colors and textures, one of Ezra's masterpieces, but he couldn't take a bite. (301–2)

Tyler's principle of impartiality toward her characters works effectively here. Probably Ezra wins this argument, not because what he says is more accurate but because he sees the futility of the question. Ezra alone cannot teach Cody to stop counting and, instead, taste the lamb and vegetables. The debate is moot.

Meanwhile, Beck leaves the banquet, and Ezra insists that the family search him out and bring him back. Cody finds Beck, who explains why he left Pearl. It was the archery set, the accident: "It was the grayness, grayness of things; half-right-and-half-wrongness of things. Everything tangled, mingled, not perfect anymore" (308). What Beck could not endure, he tells Cody, was the shortfall from his own idealizations.

Freed from the compulsion to beat time and please his

father, told at last that he is not the one responsible for his father's desertion, Cody experiences *Kairos*, a circular return to his own childhood, seen at last without his habitual distortion. Cody finally steps inside a moment— the novel's last:

> Cody held on to his elbow and led him toward the others. Overhead, seagulls drifted through a sky so clear and blue that it brought back all the outings of his boyhood—the drives, the picnics, the autumn hikes, the wildflower walks in the spring. He remembered the archery trip, and it seemed to him now that he even remembered that arrow sailing in its graceful, fluttering path. He remembered his mother's upright form along the grasses, her hair lit gold, her small hands smoothing her bouquet while the arrow journeyed on. And high above, he seemed to recall, there had been a little brown airplane, almost motionless, droning through the sunshine like a bumblebee. (319)

The arrow recalls Zeno's. It seems to move in cinemato-graphic slow motion, frame by frame, across the sky, occupying its own length, allowing Cody to step back into the moment, to see his mother from a perspective other than that of his own accusations. She sits on the grass, between the two thin vertical lines of an irreducible moment. Nevertheless, the arrow's motion is real, as it travels toward her unsuspecting shoulder; everything will follow from it.

What of the "almost motionless" airplane? It connects Cody's moment metaphorically to another instance of *Kairos*, the irreducible moment that Pearl searched for and found in her diary:

> *Early this morning . . . I went out behind the house to weed. Was kneeling in the dirt by the stable with my pinafore a mess and the perspiration rolling down my back, wiped my face on my sleeve, reached for the trowel, and all at once thought, Why I believe that at just this moment I am absolutely happy. . . .*
>
> *The Bedloe girl's piano scales were floating out her window . . . and a bottle fly was buzzing in the grass, and I saw that I was*

145

> *kneeling on such a beautiful green little planet. I don't care what else might come about, I have had this moment. It belongs to me.* (284)

Dying at eighty-five, Pearl reenters that moment; and she makes it possible, with the invitation of Beck, to allow Cody to experience the same grounding in time. The lesson they learn, now, in 1979, is the one Ezra has known all along; it is the fact of the planet, that it spins in space and time, that we ride on it for a sequence of real moments, that they can be experienced undistractedly, that there are bottle flies and airplanes about us, and that wild berries ripen in the wilderness. It is Ezra's pagan piety, his cosmic locatedness. That it took them so long to get—or relearn—the point testifies to the deep affinities between Pearl and Cody, ones that he is at last freed to confront calmly. With such knowledge available to Cody, there is the possibility that the family will finish a dinner at last, unless Beck does leave before the dessert wine is poured.

VIII *THE ACCIDENTAL TOURIST*

As her work has matured, Anne Tyler has built in-creasingly articulated metaphors out of her fascination with phobic experience. In fact, phobia, addressed clini-cally (as in, say, Alice Hoffman's *Illumination Night*), ap-pears only occasionally in her work. Instead, Tyler seems to meditate upon a phobic moment as an initial imagina-tive conception, and then to spin out fables of such elabo-rate significance that their origins all but disappear in the richness of the pattern. For instance, a very fine early short story, "Dry Water" (1965), takes as a premise a little boy's irrational fear of birds and builds from it the begin-nings of a theory of a phobic element behind aesthetic awareness. That story set the stage for the creation of Jeremy Pauling in *Celestial Navigation*, nine years later. Another story, "Outside" (1971), uses Tyler's own youthful emergence from the quiet protectiveness of a North Car-olina Quaker community to develop the character of a perceptive young man who is expert at English grammar but suffers a form of geographical dyslexia. The same combination of linguistic skill and spatial phobia troubles the Leary family in *The Accidental Tourist*. Or there is "A Flaw in the Crust of the Earth" (1967), one of the few fictions made from Tyler's Canadian sojourn in the late sixties. Its tale of a young man's panicky sense of the dangers of life in a foreign city begins the balancing act of ironies about escape and home that Charlotte Emory performs in *Earthly Possessions*.

As the phobic moment provides the premise for the complex poetics of Jeremy Pauling's art, it is also the origin of the utopian projects of the Tull children, who work free from the trauma of their mother's isolationism and rage. Thus, it is fair to say that the Tyler protagonist experiences fear as a governing emotion, and the typical Tyler plot articulates outward from an initial imagined moment of terror. In *The Accidental Tourist*, what is constructed from the phobic moment is a set of comic variations on Freud's theory of the death instincts, a funny and profound meditation on the text of *Beyond the Pleasure Principle*. We can find elements of psychic conservatism, regression, and a compulsion to repeat in earlier Tyler novels (for example, Jenny Tull's hunch that the family is doomed to return to the dinner table until they get it right). But with her tenth novel, Tyler allows Freud's dark and revolutionary speculations of 1919 to dominate her tapestry.

Macon Leary springs from a family of reclusive system-builders so vividly invoked that it is fair to name their philosophy "Learyism"—a radical distrust of the world outside the walls of their ancestral home. Abandoned by a flighty mother (another in the chain of Tyler's improvident gypsy women that includes Saul Emory's mother and Justine Peck), the Leary "children," now in their forties, live in their grandparents' house. Rose looks after the "boys" and alphabetizes her kitchen shelves. Her brothers, Porter and Charles, have both fallen out of their marriages and landed back in the house where they grew up, arguing over the subtleties of home maintenance and playing a card game only Learys can understand, called Vaccination. The novel's first hundred pages make fine comedy out of reclusion. With mastery of her material, Tyler's range has broadened, and in *The Accidental Tourist* she moves gracefully between the tragic and the downright vaudevillian.

It is in those opening hundred pages that Macon rejoins his phobia-ridden siblings. A year before the novel's opening scene, Macon's son, Ethan, had been murdered by a nineteen-year-old holdup man in a Burger Bonanza. The loss of Ethan has destroyed Macon's marriage because his wife, Sarah, suspects that the random murder of their son made no alteration in Macon's soul, that Macon's view of the world was so dark that somehow he had already assimilated such a possibility. It is his apparent calm that drives her away. As they drive home to

Baltimore from an aborted vacation, Sarah cannot persuade Macon to pull over and wait for the end of a blinding rainstorm. It would comfort her if he would, even if he does possess a "system" for driving that obviates danger. "You're not a comfort, Macon," she tells him. "I want a divorce." Macon's reversion to system, as a response to the threat of *accident*, is deeply inscribed in his character. Sarah is not privy to Macon's pain, and she does not understand the depth of compulsion that grips him. The subsequent events of the novel constitute the story of his liberation, as he learns to destroy and build anew his manner of surviving the accidentality of the world.

At the novel's beginning, Macon is a man who burrows, who does not leave home when he travels but rather extends his "safe" space by enclosing himself in familiarity. He manages to travel to London and Paris, protected against the "accidental" in a labyrinth of psychic devices. He is "encased," "muffled," "cocooned." An author of travel books for people who deeply need to stay at home, he devises systems for avoiding confrontation with anything new, unfamiliar, or foreign. He explains to his readers where they can get Chef Boy-ar-dee spaghetti in Rome. Why they should carry only a single gray suit, "in case of sudden funerals." How they should keep a long book open on their laps to avoid conversation with strangers on airplanes. (Macon carries *Miss MacIntosh*, an unfinishable novel of some nine hundred pages.) This degree of psychic conservatism is habitual, true of the baseline Macon, the man as he lived before Ethan's death.

But after Ethan dies and Sarah leaves, Macon, deprived of the opposing power of embarrassment, all alone in the world, carries the logic of his system-building into madness. He reduces his wardrobe to two sweat suits, which he launders alternately—each one every other day—by pouring detergent on them and then trampling upon them in the bathtub while he showers. He rigs feeding systems for his dog Edward and his cat Helen and connects an automatic popcorn maker to his alarm clock so that he expends minimal energy over breakfast. The conscious principles behind his venture are efficiency, energy conservation, and reduction of contact with a hostile and unfulfilling outside world. But, clearly, there are unconscious motives as well; while Tyler is no reductive Freudian, and the novel's vision is never hostage to psychoanalytic doctrine, she creates out of Macon's mad projects a boldly idiosyncratic set of musical variations, in both major and minor keys, on the theory of the death instincts.

In *Beyond the Pleasure Principle* Freud began to question his own sense of the primary status of the sexual instincts. Perhaps it was the psychic ravages of World War I, and his witnessing of the victims of combat trauma, that dramatized for him the compulsive need in human beings to reenact clearly traumatic situations. Such reenactments through dreams and repetitious behaviors could not be explained as attempts at wish-fulfillment, and they did not appear to produce pleasure. Therefore Freud postulated the existence of death instincts—as powerful and as primitive as the libidinal instincts—and he located them in the unconscious portion of the ego. Whether they were activated by adult traumas (such as combat) or by infantile traumas (the sense of threat that the Oedipal contest inspires in the child), the death instincts operated to reduce anxiety. They invoked dreams and reenactments of painful past scenes as neurotic methods for gaining mastery of dangerous stimuli, an attempt to "master the stimulus retrospectively."[1]

Freud speculated that biology might one day provide evidence that in all organic life there exists a drive to restore the organism to its earliest condition in the inorganic. Thus, in a general theoretical sense, as well as in the specific case of the trauma-induced neurosis, the force of the death instincts in all living things was conservative,

1. *The Complete Psychological Works of Sigmund Freud;* vol. 18, *Beyond the Pleasure Principle, Group Psychology, and Other Works* (London: Hogarth Press, 1955, 1968), 17, 20, 32.

a need to close off the possibility of stimuli, of any movement toward new and potentially unstable perceptions, and to repeat instead the old, the stable, and the familiar. The living organism permits a deadening of its external cortex, the interface between itself and the external world, in the interest of limiting, of walling off, stimulation, a project that Freud thought probably subsumes more of the organism's energy than perception itself.

This conservative instinctual drive manifests itself as regression. In the general sense "an instinct is an urge inherent in organic life to restore an earlier state of things which the living entity has been obliged to abandon under the pressure of external disturbing forces; that is, it is a kind of organic elasticity, or, to put it another way, the expression of the inertia inherent in organic life."[2] In the clinical context, that regression takes the form of a return to childhood.

Macon Leary doubly personifies Freud's speculations. First, he is inscribed in the book in a series of cartoon illustrations of Freud's general theory of the death instincts, providing Tyler with an opportunity to play on the funnier, Bergsonian aspects of compulsion. At this level, the reader is invited to share in Sarah's incomplete vision of Macon. But he is more than a comic diagram, a series of psychiatric gags. Tyler also renders him in a convincing clinical context, and this endeavor approaches tragedy. Macon's regressiveness and psychic conservatism were established long before the loss of Ethan, in consequence of the inconsistent child-rearing of his flighty mother, Alicia. Then, with Ethan's death, Macon suffers an adult trauma-induced neurosis, his regressiveness turns acute, and he unconsciously starts dreaming (at varied levels of censorship) and neurotically repeating the moment in the morgue when he confronted the corpse of his murdered son.

Sarah's abandonment of him drives Macon a little mad. Sane in terms of its own premises, Macon's compulsive

2. Ibid., 36.

151

routine makes him wretched, and he finds himself unable to sleep. Tyler provides the reader with a detailed account of Macon's thoughts during one of his frequent bouts of insomnia. No matter how he begins his treacherous nightly slide into the preconscious, Macon's ideas gravitate toward Ethan:

> Ethan went away to camp when he was twelve—a year ago, almost exactly. Most boys started earlier, but Macon had kept delaying it. Why have a child at all, he asked Sarah, if you were only going to ship him off to some godforsaken spot in Virginia? By the time he finally gave in, Ethan was in the top age group—a tall blond sprout of a boy with an open, friendly face and an endearing habit of bouncing on the balls of his feet when he was nervous.
>
> Don't think about it.[3]

That last sentence is repeated when Macon's mind slides toward Ethan again. Macon ends up getting up every night and going downstairs. Sometimes he looks out his windows in the wee hours and takes comfort in finding a light on in another house, someone else "sitting up wide awake fending off his thoughts" (20).

Macon cannot allow himself to remember Ethan in the morgue or imagine the moment in which the nineteen-year-old fired the pistol into the back of Ethan's head. He can avoid dreaming the event by interrupting his sleep. But he does not see that he is repeating Ethan's death in his own compulsive actions. His mad housekeeping systems are coded disinterments of Ethan. For example, Macon decides to sew up the bed sheets into sleeping bags: "What he did was strip the mattress of all linens, replacing them with a giant sort of envelope made from one of the seven sheets he had folded and stitched together on the sewing machine. He thought of this invention as a Macon Leary Body Bag. A body bag required no tucking in, was unmussable, easily changeable, and the

3. *The Accidental Tourist* (New York: Alfred A. Knopf, 1985), 18. Hereafter cited parenthetically in the text by page number.

perfect weight for summer nights" (11). What Macon does not remember, in his celebration of its efficiency, is where he last saw such a garment.

Eventually, Macon's system breaks down. He reconnects the dryer exhaust hose to the dryer, forgetting that it is now the cat's route in the basement window. Trapped, the cat lets out an ungodly howl. On the basement steps, effecting her rescue, Macon trips over the skateboard that has become his laundry cart and breaks his leg. Then, when he gets out of the hospital, he moves into the Leary family house where his sister and brothers have already regathered. It is the act of regression that—short of death itself—he has been longing for. In his grandparent's house, "Macon leaned back in his chair with his coffee mug cupped in both hands. The sun was warming the breakfast table, and the kitchen smelled of toast. He almost wondered whether, by some devious, subconscious means, he had engineered this injury—every elaborate step leading up to it—just so he could settle down safe among the people he'd started out with" (63). It is one of the sadder ironies of the novel that Macon and Sarah are well-educated people who can speak fluent Freudian. Yet Macon, while he can wonder at the mysteries of his motivation, cannot heal himself, and Sarah, who has ceased to find him "mysterious," mistakes his compulsion for coldness.

Once Macon has returned to the family home, he naturally enjoys the immobility of his broken leg, and he envisions its absolute form: "It was hard for him to imagine resuming his travels. Sometimes he wished he could stay in his cast forever. In fact, he wished it covered him from head to foot. People would thump faintly on his chest. They'd peer through his eyeholes. 'Macon? You in there?' Maybe he was, maybe he wasn't. No one would ever know" (125). This is, of course, another play on Freud's speculative concept of the cortex, which is, after all, an organic body cast, an exoskeleton. Freud wrote: "By its death, the outer layer has saved all the deeper layers from a similar fate—unless, that is to say, stimuli reach it which are so strong that they break through the protective

153

shield."[4] But there is also in a specific sense something truly terrible about Macon's fantasy. It is an unconscious attempt at repetition. When his life with Muriel Pritchett finally restores Macon to the point that he can remember the moment when he half-emptied his lungs and entered the room to identify Ethan, he recalls that he told Sarah that what he saw was *an empty shell:* "Odd how clear it suddenly became, once a person had died, that the body was the very least of him. This was simply an untenanted shell, although it bore a distant resemblance to Ethan" (315). His entire life's undertaking, in the aftermath of his son's death, has been to regress toward the nonliving, to reproduce the corpse in himself.

Sarah is forgivable in seeing only the surface, the shell, of Macon's "appalling calm." His rationality infuriated her when, shortly after the trip to the morgue, she had demanded to know what he saw:

> Macon said, "Sarah. Listen. I will tell you as much as I can. He was very pale and still. You wouldn't believe how still. He didn't have any expression. His eyes were closed. There was nothing bloody or gruesome, just a sense of . . . futility. I mean I wondered what the purpose had been. His arms were down by his sides and I thought about last spring when he started lifting weights. I thought, 'Is this what it comes to? Lift weights and take vitamins and build yourself up and then—nothing?' "
>
> He hadn't been prepared for Sarah's response. "So what are you saying?" she asked him. "We die in the end, so why bother to live in the first place? Is that what you're saying?"
>
> "No—" he said.
>
> "It all comes down to a question of economy?" she asked.
>
> "No, Sarah. Wait," he had said. (316–17)

Required to think and speak of an event that has injured him below the levels of thought and speech, Macon reverts to the macrocosmic, to a generalized pessimism, and he echoes Freud's bleakest sentences. Freud opens

4. Freud, *Beyond the Pleasure Principle,* 27.

Beyond the Pleasure Principle by saying, "We are introducing an economic point of view into our work." Later he states, "If we are to take it as a truth that knows no exception that everything living dies for internal reasons—becomes inorganic once again—then we shall be compelled to say that *'The aim of all life is death'* and looking backwards, that *inanimate things existed before animate ones*."[5] Asked if that is really what he meant, that it is all a question of economy, that the aim of life is death, Macon said "No." But his sincere act of denial has no force—it requires an unpacking that subsequent events in the book must effect. At this point Macon does not understand his own oddity: he is a man who grieves through ideas of economy, weeps via acts of efficiency.

Freud envisioned analysis as the work of carrying the neurotic patient from a condition in which he dreams and compulsively repeats the content of his trauma to a condition in which he remembers it. The therapeutic mechanism of "transference-neurosis" permits the patient to reenact the painful but repressed past and redirect emotions at the analyst that were previously directed elsewhere—in the case of infantile trauma, at a parent. Then, an occasion arises in which the patient has an opportunity to acknowledge the repressed content consciously, understand it, and work free of its control. It is in this sense that the plot of *Accidental Tourist* is structured as an extended process of *anamnesis,* a therapeutic movement.

The improbable "therapist" who carries Macon through a successful transference neurosis is a dog trainer by the name of Muriel Pritchett. Ethan's death has also caused a psychic disturbance in his dog, a Welsh corgi named Edward, who, through a piece of novelistic wizardry on Tyler's part, comes to embody Macon's own unconscious. When Edward starts attacking strangers and refusing to allow Learys to leave the house, Macon reluctantly phones Muriel and asks her to train his dog. He finds Muriel "bizarre." She wears garish evening clothes in the day-

5. Ibid., 7, 38.

time and speaks a demotic, ungrammatical English. She is transparently interested in Macon as a potential husband and unsuccessfully hides from him the fact that she has an asthmatic little boy from a disastrous early marriage.

Yet Macon admires her resourcefulness and sheer strength of will. (She tells him the story of a Doberman who knocked her off a porch, broke her arm, and stood snarling over her. "Absolutely not!" she had said, and the dog backed off.) Slowly and skeptically, Macon is drawn to her, but then he finds he cannot accept her invitation to dinner. He drives to her house in a poor area of downtown Baltimore to leave an explanatory note. She opens the door, and he has to speak the words that until that moment he had avoided:

> "I lost my son," Macon said. "He was just . . . he went to a hamburger joint and then . . . someone came, a holdup man, and shot him. I can't go to dinner with people! I can't talk to their little boys! You have to stop asking me. I don't mean to hurt your feelings but I'm just not up to this, do you hear?"
>
> She took one of his wrists very gently and she drew him into the house, still not fully opening the door, so that he had a sense of slipping through something, of narrowly evading something. She closed the door behind them. She put her arms around him and hugged him. (199–200)

Muriel leads him upstairs, puts him to bed, and tells him to sleep. Later, after she has climbed in with him:

> She sighed in her sleep and lifted his hand and placed it upon her stomach. The robe had fallen open; he felt smooth skin, and then a corrugated ridge of flesh jutting across her abdomen. The Caesarean, he thought. And it seemed to him, as he sank back into his dreams, that she had as good as spoken aloud. *About your son,* she seemed to be saying: *Just put your hand here. I'm scarred too. We're all scarred. You are not the only one.* (201)

156

Like Elizabeth Abbot in *The Clock Winder,* Muriel is magically empowered to heal people, but she is less chary of her talent. And her actions toward Macon neatly parallel the role of the therapist in a transference neurosis. First, in his regressiveness, Macon longs so deeply for maternal comforts that he has had to acknowledge to a degree the nature of his need. At the top of the World Trade Center, he suffers a panic attack (not acrophobia, he sees, but loss of connectedness). Starved for a "mere human touch," Macon finds himself on the verge of speaking to a strange woman in the lobby: "Excuse me, Ma'am, I wonder if you would be so kind as to, um . . . but the only request that came to mind rose up from his earliest childhood: *Carry me!*" (161). Macon then swiftly rationalizes an excuse to phone Muriel instead, so that she can satisfy this maternal need. Macon had also felt childish impulses to punish Sarah for leaving him, as if she were repeating the untrustworthiness of his actual mother. And he joins his brothers, Porter and Charles, in relying on their sister, Rose, as a mother surrogate in their retreat from adult life in the Leary refuge.

Thus going to bed with Muriel is initially a regressive act that allows Macon to confront the need for warmth and nourishment that his systematic defenses have disguised. The cesarean scar as maternal wound first marks Muriel as a mother for Macon, but it also signals a recovery at the end of regression. Through it, Muriel informs him that there are also wounds that support life, that are suffered in brave opposition to the world's accidentality. Muriel's scar repeats the wound that Macon could not bear to see but wants to inflict on himself, Ethan's: "He had followed a man into a room. It was not as bad as it could have been because someone had folded a wad of towelling under the back of Ethan's head to hide the damage" (315). Muriel's body may be skinny and unluxurious, but it is also open, available, and without the morgue's decorum: she frequently forgets to keep her skimpy robe closed, a worry for Macon when Porter visits. Muriel provides a transference for Macon, supplying both the womb and the scar that he must reexperience to free himself of compulsion.

Muriel succeeds, and soon Macon is transformed under her influence: "In the foreign country that was Singleton Street he was an entirely different person. This person had never been suspected of narrowness, never been accused of chilliness; in fact, was mocked for his soft heart. And he was anything but orderly" (212). Aware of her own therapeutic powers, Muriel worries. She wants a husband, not a patient who, once he is healed, needs her no longer. (Freud saw the decline of intimacy between patient and therapist as the sign of a cure.) Muriel tells Macon about a man with whom she had been involved who, betrayed by his wife, distrusted all women:

"But bit by bit I changed all that. He relaxed. He got to be a whole different man. Moved in with me and took over the bills, paid off all I still owed Alexander's doctor. We started talking about getting married. Then he met an airline stewardess and eloped with her within the week."

"I see," Macon said.

"It was like I had, you know, cured him, just so he could elope with another woman." (273)

It happens again. Macon does leave Muriel and return to Sarah, but then his final choice of Muriel as his wife marks a transcendence of the terms of their connection. When Macon goes back to Muriel at the novel's end, it is the emotional choice of a free man, not an unconscious regressive lurch.

That moment in which Muriel places Macon's hand on her stomach is worth a second look, because it contains something that is central to the novel's technique, as well as its vision of survival in an accidental world. Tyler wrote: "The Caesarean, he thought. And it seemed to him, as he sank back into his dreams, that she had as good as spoken aloud." Muriel's message—"*We're all scarred*"—occurs in the text in italics, but the words are unspoken. (Note that the same thing happens with Macon's plea to the lady in the restaurant, "*Carry me!*" It is a consistent principle of the novel's composition that direct and powerful emotions do not emerge in speech.) Tyler shows a Sternean commitment to the sentimental idea that valid feeling is a thing of the body and is conveyed in gesture.

Muriel's verbal inarticulateness and her dreadful English usage signal an incommensurability between valid emotion and proper speech. This is a long-standing prejudice in Tyler's fiction, a pastoral myth of the authenticity of lower-class, regionally bound people, whose lives are more vivid than those of her deracinated sophisticates. Muriel's speech is a source of comedy and vivid characterization. Tyler's ear is perfect, and Muriel's language is a plausible combination of working-class Baltimore and international valley girl. She peppers her sentences with ungrammatical "like's"; she says "disinterested" for "uninterested," "eck cetera," and "a-nother" as in "a-totally-nother person." (This is, of course, exactly what Macon becomes.) Her speech places her in schematic opposition to the compulsively well-spoken Learys, who resort gleefully to the dictionary for arbitration, who enthusiastically lament the decline of American diction, and who energetically correct outsiders' solecisms.

Yet memories of Muriel, despite her vulgarity, cut Macon's consciousness like a knife, while a bland familiarity makes Sarah nearly invisible to him—her well-chosen words, suspended in their perfect syntax, become muffled, pointless, and even annoying: "Really, Macon, you don't even communicate when you communicate." "'Oh communicate.' It was Macon's least favorite word" (137).[6]

The Learys combine a highly articulate use of language with geographical dyslexia. Never at a loss for words, they are often lost in Baltimore, and the simplest trip to the hardware store can have them circling blocks for hours. Muriel, on the other hand, runs an errand busi-

6. It is also one of Tyler's. See her wry comment quoted on pp. 68–69, above.

ness that exploits her canny sense of the city. In *The Accidental Tourist*, spatial orientation, as opposed to linguistic sophistication, is a metaphor for engagement, the ability to step into the accidental world and continue breathing. Muriel's grounded speech and sense of location are in turn tied to her fearlessness. ("I'm not afraid of a thing in this world," she tells Macon.) She is magically adroit as a dog trainer because she is so fiercely connected to the mortal world. In the interlocked significances of the novel, her power over Macon's dog Edward signifies her ability to penetrate to his subconscious, to pierce the mummy wraps of ritual and language that he has wound so deliberately.

One happy consequence of Tyler's celebration of unspoken feeling in the novel is that it allows a dog to become a major character. Not surprisingly, Edward's actions constitute gestures deeper than language. Macon discusses Edward with Muriel:

"But this is just the simplest problem. His only fault is, he wants to protect me."

"You can take protection too far," Muriel told him.

Macon tried a little joke. "'It's a jungle out there,' he's saying. That's what he's trying to say. 'I know better than you do, Macon.'"

"Oh?" Muriel said. "You let him call you by your first name?" (97)[7]

Obviously, Muriel is fluent in unspoken language in ways Macon only begins to imagine. She explains, "When they

7. As the Leary dog, Edward has a name that is very close to that of Edward Lear, the famous human agoraphobe, nonsense poet, and author of a series of travel sketches formulaically entitled *An Itinerant Artist in. . . .* Lear wrote limericks that swiftly sum up his canine namesake's view of humanity. One must suffice here:

There was an Old Person of Basing,
Whose presence of mind was amazing;
He purchased a steed, which he rode at full speed,
And escaped from the people of Basing.

lick their lips it's good, but when they put their foot on top of your foot it's bad." "Sounds like a secret language, just about doesn't it?" (123). But it is a fierce language, spoken in the land of accident, and its subject is often the exercise of will. Muriel shocks Macon when she lifts a recalcitrant Edward off the ground and briefly hangs him by his leash. When Macon balks at such violence, Muriel asks him if he wants a dog that "hates the whole world. That wants to kill the whole world." "'Why yes, I guess you do,' she said" (123).

Slowly, she changes that, and as she transforms both dog and owner, they gravitate naturally toward Singleton Street, looking for lessons in a foreign language. Muriel's family is quarrelsome, her house disorderly, and her son, Alexander, is a frightened little boy with many allergies and no friends. But, with no husband and almost no money, Muriel has worked out elaborate cooperative arrangements with her neighbors and her landlord for shelter, transportation, and baby-sitting. And she sustains half-a-dozen part-time jobs. Singleton Street is a model of unidealized vitality, and Tyler's sentimental myth is plausibly conveyed. Her earlier sketches of working-class people accented their zany insouciance but never quite took them seriously. Singleton Street is Tyler's first fully realized invention of characters who do not have enough money. And the death of Muriel's teenage neighbor, Dommie Sadler, is an acknowledgment of the power of accident over unaccommodated people that earlier novels did not quite make.

Macon admits to a degree of embarrassment concerning his liaison; frequently in the novel he sees himself through the eyes of his mocking employer, Julian Edge, or of his brothers, who suspect that, in Muriel and Alexander, Macon is looking for a substitute family and that this one is of inferior stock. Macon learns to risk absurdity for things that are more important, and it is Edward who clarifies his sense of things. When he finally moves in with Muriel, Macon brings Edward to the house, and they discover that Alexander is not so severely allergic to dogs after all. In fact, the novel quietly and credibly marks the stages in Alexander's blossoming under the influence of Macon and his dog:

> For the first few hours they tried to keep him in a separate part of the house, which of course was hopeless. He had to follow Macon wherever he went, and also he developed an immediate interest in Alexander. Lacking a ball, he kept dropping small objects at Alexander's feet and then stepping back to look expectantly into his face. "He wants to play fetch," Macon explained. Alexander picked up a matchbox and tossed it, angling his arm behind him in a prissy way. While Edward went tearing after it, Macon made a mental note to buy a ball first thing in the morning and teach Alexander how to throw. (232)

This is among the most significant of those unspoken messages in a book that rests its movement upon them. In fact, in Tyler's plot design, this unspoken message is climactic. Edward substitutes matchbox for ball, Alexander for Ethan. The act is his silent homiletic, directed at his master. The reader is invited to infer its content, which would go something like this: *Macon, I am a dog. I require a little boy. Ethan is dead. You and I are still alive.* It is a tribute to Tyler's novelistic powers that a dog could so plausibly possess—and convey—that wisdom.

In the first year following Ethan's death, Macon could not heed Edward's message. It requires as a prerequisite Muriel Pritchet's course in the unavoidability of accident. To Macon, searching for a substitute son is embarrassing because it forces him to a public admission of his emotional need. He overcomes that embarrassment when he bumps into his former mother-in-law while buying clothes for Alexander at a shopping mall. But there is an even greater obstruction. Macon finds it hard to start over with outsiders, strangers, people whom accident has cast in his path. Yet, as Muriel's powers work upon him, Macon accepts the fact that there was something tentative about being Ethan's real parent in the first place. It is easier to

162

accept a substitute when one ceases to idealize the past and remembers that one's "original" life was never above the accidental:

> Once when Ethan was little, not more than two or three, he had run out into the street after a ball. Macon had been too far away to stop him. All he could do was shout, "No!" and then watch, frozen with horror, as a pickup truck came barreling around the curve. In that instant, he released his claim. In one split second he adjusted to a future that held no Ethan—an immeasurably bleaker place but also, by way of compensation, plainer and simpler, free of the problems a small child trails along with him, the endless demands and the mess and the contests for his mother's attention. Then the truck stopped short and Ethan retrieved the ball, and Macon's knees went weak with relief. But he remembered forever after how quickly he had adjusted. (143)

The thought that encouraged Macon's compulsions during Ethan's life returns to free him of them after Ethan's death. There is no safety, no order. In that light, Macon begins to rethink travel—Tyler's metaphor for immersion in the accidental. Macon discovers that San Francisco is beautiful. (San Francisco is the city where even non-phobic visitors find themselves subject to odd bouts of apprehension.) He feels a little ashamed for making a phobic protégé of one of his readers, Lucas Loomis. He coaches Mrs. Daniel Bunn through an attack of air-travel terror and then feels oddly competent. Muriel trails him to Paris and breaks all the rules in his guidebook. The Parisians are friendly; she finds bargains; the water is salubrious. He was wrong. Then, on a night flight, he dreams he is sitting next to the fictional Miss MacIntosh—that personification of deathly self-enclosure. Fittingly, she offers him a silent rebuke, for he has left her company forever.

As Macon learns to locate himself in the accidental world, he begins to change his thinking about time. In his compulsive stage, when he had to travel, he set his digital clock to the time of his destination but kept his watch with the circular hands set at Baltimore time. "Real time" he called it. But one sign that he is cured is his newly won capacity to think of all times as relative and of all persons as equally adrift in an arbitrary but possibly endurable world. In turn, the thought allows him to envision Ethan differently. Perhaps Ethan ages as well, his time as "real" as that of the living:

> And if dead people aged, wouldn't it be a comfort? To think of Ethan growing up in heaven—fourteen years old now instead of twelve—eased the grief a little. Oh, it was their immunity to time that made the dead so heartbreaking. . . . Macon gazed out the cab window, considering the notion in his mind. He felt a kind of inner rush, a racing forward. The real adventure, he thought, is the flow of time; it's as much adventure as anyone could wish. And if he pictured Ethan still part of that flow—in some other place, however unreachable—he believed he might be able to bear it after all. (354)

Macon has reversed his terms: instead of trying to establish a condition apart from time and accident, he imaginatively draws Ethan back into them.

IX BREATHING LESSONS

IN a goofy moment at the nursing home where she works as an aide, Maggie Moran, the heroine of Anne Tyler's eleventh novel, *Breathing Lessons*, has to climb out of a laundry cart and face her angry supervisor. The hope flashes through Maggie's mind that she will be mistaken for an "*I love Lucy* type—madcap, fun-loving, full of irrepressible high spirits."[1] Then, quickly, she admits to herself that she never liked *I Love Lucy*, with its excessive contrivances and impossible plots. In the manner of many women of her generation, though, Maggie seems compelled to cultivate a set of gestures that signal her personal inconsequence. By means of a series of conscious decisions, made over decades, Maggie, in her midforties, has become dizzy, overemotional, meddling, and, on the surface of it, an intellectual lightweight.

Breathing Lessons opens with an announcement of her blandly comic susceptibility to pratfall. Initially, Tyler sets up, in a farcical scene in front of an auto-repair shop, the same combination of accident-prone protagonist and unmanageable physical universe that colored the first hundred pages of *The Accidental Tourist*. Then, as she did with Macon, Tyler pilots Maggie into deeper emotional waters.

In *Breathing Lessons*, though, Tyler undertakes a new experiment in lyric modes. She employs the easily accessible sitcom vocabulary of domestic fiction—dented fenders, home movies, and beer-stein collections—and casts it in a syntax that achieves a nobly restrained, almost abstract quality. The texts most immediately present in *Breathing Lessons* are popular: first the sentimental songs of Maggie and her husband Ira's generation of the fifties,

1. *Breathing Lessons* (New York: Alfred A. Knopf, 1988), 45. Hereafter cited parenthetically in the text by page number.

"Que Sera, Sera," and "Love Is a Many Splendored Thing"; then their son's sadly jaundiced, cosmically disappointed music of the late seventies, Iggy Pop and Canned Heat. Out of these, and the loss of the culture's innocence that they record, Tyler crafts more complicated emotions. *Breathing Lessons* grows into a book in which skies darken, birds twitter and then descend on the horizon, and, though it is merely September, winter impends. Maggie, in her ubiquity and her blowsy distractedness, approaches the mythic sufficiency of Keats's figure of Autumn. She attains a serenity that Tyler suggests with the novel's title and sustains subtly through the rhythms of its sentences. Breathing, the involuntary act that ties us to the specific, physical moment, is also subject to calm, voluntary control. With middle age, the capacity for surprise is muted by redundancy.

It is redundancy that governs the novel's design. *Breathing Lessons* recounts a day in the life of the Morans, as they drive from their shopkeeping section of Baltimore to Deer Lick, Pennsylvania, to attend the funeral of Max Gill, the husband of Maggie's best friend from high school, Serena. Apparently a little hysterical at Max's death, Serena demands that all her old friends attend the funeral and replay the roles they had taken at her innovative wedding. When Ira stolidly refuses to rise and sing his part in his and Maggie's duet of "Love Is a Many Splendored Thing," Durwood Klegg stands, sings Ira's part, and rescues Maggie from her wobbly solo. Then, at the reception after the memorial service, Serena shows a home movie of her and Max's wedding. The home movie allows a second measure of time's insolence, as the guests view faded and flickering eight-millimeter images of themselves, silently warbling their assigned tunes from thirty-year-younger faces. The other guests all hum along, the heard melodies being sweet enough for them.

For Maggie, though, the film elicits a response deeper than nostalgia. Her singing of that duet with Ira had occurred only moments after she had gone to his picture-frame shop, where the two of them had defied Ira's parasitic father, agreed to marry, and embraced for the first time. Thus the film before Maggie's eyes is an object for Keatsian contemplation. It shows her a pair of lovers caught in the immediate aftermath of a significant moment of passion. Thirty years later, she finds herself having slipped away from it, caught in time's irreversibility, awash in ordinariness.

Middle age, Tyler insists, holds a redundancy of such mirrors, or memories. As her Spenserian, allegorical name suggests, Serena has organized this day as a message specifically for Maggie, who seems to be going through all the stages of her own life, from first menstruation to menopause, and perhaps eventually widowhood, one step behind her friend. Serena's lesson is one in "letting go," and she opens Maggie's moral education with an introductory lecture on the subject of relinquishment: Maggie and Ira's son, Jesse, a failing rock musician, has married and divorced a young woman named Fiona Stuckey; since Fiona walked out, Maggie has fiercely missed her granddaughter, Leroy, now seven.

"Oh, Maggie, let her go," Serena said. "Let it all go! That's what I say. I was watching Linda's boys this morning, climbing our back fence, and first I thought, Oh-oh, better call them in; they're bound to rip those sissy little suits, and then I thought, Nah, forget it. It's not *my* affair, I thought. Let them go."

"But I don't want to let go," Maggie said. "What kind of talk is that?"

"You don't have any choice," Serena told her. She stepped over a branch that lay across their path. "That's what it comes down to in the end, willy-nilly: just pruning and disposing. Why, you've been doing that all along, right? You start shucking off your children from the day you give birth; that's the whole point. A big, big moment is when you can look at them and say, 'Now if I died they could get along without me. I'm free to die,' you say. 'What a relief!' Discard, discard! Throw out the toys in the basement. Move to a smaller house. Menopause delighted me." (80)

Wisely, Maggie rejects Serena's sardonic posture and ultimately comes to a subtler appreciation of the destiny nature holds for her. But her initial impulse is not refinement but rebellion, and she sneaks into Serena's bedroom after the home movie and seduces Ira, who had dealt himself a hand of solitaire on Serena's vanity table. Serena interrupts them at the zipper-pulling stage and expels them from her Bower of Bitter Acceptance, but not before Maggie gets to assert her vitality. Maggie is—and wants it known that she is—ripe, not rotten, and there is nothing lugubrious in her resistance to loneliness and premature dereliction.

Serena's general intention was to read to all her friends a lecture on mortality, to perform a brief *danse macabre*. Max, at only fifty, had suffered metastasis before the doctor had even diagnosed cancer. Suddenly, one day quite close to the end of his life, he wandered away and a neighbor had to lead him home. Serena ponders the effects of that disorientation—caused by a brain tumor—and then designs a funeral to ensure that, in milder form, it will reoccur in the minds of her guests:

> "What would it be like, I wonder," Serena said. "Just to look around you one day and have it all amaze you—where you'd arrived at, who you'd married, what kind of person you'd grown into. Say you suddenly came to while you were—oh, say, out shopping with your daughter—but it was your seven or eight-year-old self observing all you did. 'Why!' you'd say. 'Can this be me? Driving a car? Taking charge? Nagging some young woman like I knew what I was doing?' You'd walk into your house and say, 'Well, I don't think all that much of my taste.' You'd go to a mirror and say, 'Goodness, my chin is starting to slope just the way my mother's did.' I mean you'd be looking at things without their curtains. You'd say, 'My husband isn't any Einstein, is he?' (53)

So Serena constructs a ceremony that provides precisely those rueful pleasures, setting up two redundant mirrors on the past she shared with Maggie (the songfest, the home movie) so that Maggie must, before the day ends, pull away some "curtains." The novel's narrative structure mirrors, but also elaborates upon and qualifies, Serena's ritual. The single day of the narrative contains Maggie and Ira's journey to Deer Lick; their detour to visit Fiona, Jesse's ex-wife; and their attempt to bring Fiona and Leroy back to Baltimore in hopes of a reconciliation. But it is a day fraught with recollection, and Tyler uses a bold subjective flashback technique, a following of memories triggered by the day's events, allowing those memories a rhythm and a duration all their own, each act of retrospection mirroring the present and measuring losses sustained.

There is the story of Maggie and Ira's own courtship, with its due quantity of inadvertence—Maggie only found her way to Ira because she heard he was dead and tried to console his father. There is Jessie getting Fiona "into trouble" and Maggie persuading Fiona to keep the baby—which culminates in a scene outside an abortion clinic, in which Maggie simultaneously dissuades Fiona and battles off anti-abortion picketers. Also, there are vignettes of Ira's family—his broken-down dad and two sisters, one retarded, one agoraphobic—on an unsuccessful outing to Baltimore's civic Disneyland, Harbor Place, and on their annual trip to Pimlico racetrack, the scene that broke the frail bond of Jesse and Fiona's marriage.

The novel divides into a three-part form to contain the day and the retrospections it evokes. Part one, comprising three chapters, is in Maggie's consciousness and contains the events of the morning. Pratfall predominates. Maggie backs into a truck in front of the repair shop; then she loses the map and Serena's directions to Deer Lick. She enters into a heart-to-heart talk with a coffee-shop waitress, then, back on the road, quarrels with the stolid Ira about her lack of reticence, gets out of the car, and decides to leave him once and for all. He comes back for her, they attend the memorial service, and part one ends with their expulsion from Serena's bedroom.

Part two is in Ira's mind, a single chapter of memories evoked while he is at the wheel. This *entr'acte*, in which the day's events do not move forward, possesses a power-ful emotional dynamic, as the initial coldness of Ira's observation breaks up like an ice floe, and the buried *Menschlichkeit* of this disappointed solitaire addict carries all before it.

Finally, part three is Maggie's once again. It records the meandering journey homeward, including a misadventure with a slow-driving elderly black man named Mr. Otis. Maggie then talks Ira into visiting Fiona and persuades her to pack a bag and take Leroy for a visit in Baltimore. On the way, they stop at a grocery to pick up supplies; when the musak plays a song from 1956, "Tonight You Belong to Me" by Patience and Prudence, Maggie and Ira finally sing the duet that Ira had refused to be part of at the funeral. Part three ends back in the Morans' bedroom, Fiona and Leroy's visit having ended in disaster. "Oh, Ira," Maggie says, dropping down beside him, "what are we two going to live for, all the rest of our lives?" (326). As with part two, this final section is fraught with memory, completing the rich evocation of time and its power—like that of wind or water on the earth—to shape and erode a marriage.

Maggie's moment of quiet desperation is elicited by the day, of course, and the memories it evoked, but also by a phone call to Serena in which she gained Serena's forgiveness for her and Ira's horny disrespect for the dead. In return, though, Maggie is plagued with a memory of the time she helped put Serena's mother in the nursing home where Maggie works as a nurse's aide. Maggie had assumed there was to be a costume party on Halloween night, and so she had wheeled Serena's mother on her maiden voyage into the residents' lounge dressed in a clown suit, wearing a fright wig, and restrained in her wheelchair with a posy. The woman needed months to recover from the humiliation.

The situation is one that must repeat Tyler's worst anxieties about Maggie, who is aging and who verges, repeatedly, on clownishness. Tyler makes "a character" of Maggie. She mangles the car twice in one day by stupidly panicking at the wheel. On a third occasion, she grabs the wheel from Ira and runs them into a ditch. She tells her life story to strangers and seduces her husband at a funeral. But, on the surface of things, Maggie's worst foolishness lies in her tendency to meddle. She stopped Fiona—who is highly susceptible to gesture—from having the abortion by telling her Jesse was building a handmade crib for their baby. She persuades Fiona to come to Baltimore seven years later by insisting that Jesse has kept her soap box in his bedroom for the smell of her. Ira explains Maggie's impulses correctly: "It's Maggie's weakness: She believes it's all right to alter people's lives. She thinks the people she loves are better than they really are, and so then she starts changing things around to suit her view of them" (270).

Ira is both Maggie's opposite and her complement, but the resulting partnership has friction to it, and schematism does not imply facility. Ira is laconic and self-enclosed, and he repeatedly wounds his family—especially Jesse—by pointing to precisely those fraying fibers of truth that Maggie wants to weave into new tapestries. In any idle moment—and the novel is designed to produce many—Maggie will launch into autobiography, in an attempt to extract significance from her story. Ira, defeated in that enterprise, will lay out a game of solitaire. Reviewers of *Breathing Lessons* have seen in this opposition evidence of a "troubled" marriage. Yet it is alien to Tyler's imagination to separate out the "pathological" from the "normal," and the powerfully elegiac tone of the novel disallows any reading that attempts to set Maggie and Ira aside as a clinical case, worse off than any other middle-aged couple, less susceptible to available joys.

Ira's iciness is a case in point. Part two of the novel, exactly fifty pages long in the Knopf edition, begins, "For the past several months now, Ira had been noticing the human race's wastefulness. People were squandering their lives, it seemed to him. They were splurging their energies on petty jealousies or vain ambitions or long-standing, bitter grudges" (125). Yet the sequence of memories that Serena's ceremony and Maggie's eroticism evoke in his mind diverts his section into lyricism. Ira makes brutally frank self-assessments, and he *has* sunk into ordinariness. He did not go to college and then medical school, but stayed home to support his family. He has spent his adult life cutting mitered corners for frames for needlework pictures of pet cats. His last memory, triggered by haze on his windshield—a haze that, like fog, evokes the autumnal in both him and Maggie—is of his sisters, Junie and Dorrie, his abdicated father, who dropped all the reins of responsibility the day Ira graduated from high school, and Maggie, on that pleasure mission to Harbor Place. It was foggy; there were no people; Dorrie had become obsessed with Mylar balloons. Remorseful at having impatiently punctured Dorrie's addled worship of Elvis Presley, he had put his arm around her shivering frame.

> And Junie had pressed close to his other side and Maggie and Sam had watched steadfastly, waiting for him to say what to do next. He had known then what the truth was; Lord, yes. It was not his having to support these people but his failure to notice how he loved them. He loved even his worn-down, defeated father, even the memory of his poor mother who had always been so pretty and never realized it because any time she approached a mirror she had her mouth drawn up lopsided with shyness.
>
> But then the feeling had faded (probably the very next instant, when Junie started begging to leave) and he forgot what he had learned. And no doubt he would forget again, just as Dorrie had forgotten, by the time she reached home, that Elvis Presley was no longer King of Rock. (175)

Of such ordinary materials, Tyler daringly demonstrates, can autumnals be made. Ira's portion of the poetic labor of this novel is made even more difficult by the fact that he does not talk. (Tyler began tucking emotion under laconism in *Tin Can Tree* and perfected her use of the unspoken line of emotional truth—"it was as if she had spoken aloud"—in *The Accidental Tourist*.) *Breathing Lessons* gains its darkest tones from Ira's silences. It is in part three, after Fiona's visit has failed and Maggie and Ira are left alone in the kitchen, that his deepest feelings get recorded. Wordless, they nevertheless validate the emotion behind Maggie's garrulity. Opening a can of soup whose label says it contains two-and-three-quarters servings, Maggie breaks down at the absence of integers; the label suggests the reduced numbers at her own table, the dwindling of opportunities to feed. She looks up and finds Ira slumped over the dining table. She wonders what has upset him:

> The answer seemed to arrive through his back—through the ripple of knobby vertebrae down his C-shaped, warm, thin back. Her fingers felt the answer first.
> He was just as sad as Maggie was, and for just the same reasons. He was lonely and tired and lacking in hope and his son had not turned out well and his daughter didn't think much of him, and he still couldn't figure out where he had gone wrong.
> He let his head fall against her shoulder. His hair was thick and rough, strung through with threads of gray that she had never noticed before, that pierced her heart in a way that her own few gray hairs never had. She hugged him tightly and nuzzled her face against his cheekbone. She said, "It will be all right. It will be all right." (280–81)

This moment, as with Ira's tendency to reveal himself inadvertently through the tunes he whistles, marks the latest stage in Tyler's most sustained utopian project, a system of gesture that silently expresses the heart's music before the brain can meddle. For the brain is a compulsive idealizer. Like the Morans' daughter, Daisy, it will go looking for "Mrs. Perfect," find her, and decide that one's own home is too squabbly and shabby to endure. In *Breathing Lessons*, it is the heart's language that is valid, but in Ira it is subjected to considerable constraint, sinking into silence. In Maggie, on the other hand, it risks folly.

Tyler's metaphor for the Morans' marriage is the duet. Sometimes they do not sing—as when, at the funeral, Ira refuses. Other times they do—as in their specious optimism when they are with Fiona and Leroy at the grocery store. (Even there, Maggie breaks it off because "all at once she imagined some deception in this scene, some lie that she and Ira were collaborating in with their compliant harmonizing and the romantic gaze they trained upon each other," 296). The narrative structure of the novel reproduces the duet form by dividing the reportage of the day's retrospections between Maggie and Ira, so that, just as at Serena and Max's wedding twenty-nine years before, they start out together, then each take a verse, then end together. The fact that this narrative arrangement captures is that no marriage can be measured from outside, or even from within. Maggie is shocked that Fiona thinks of her and Ira as constantly arguing and inharmonious, whereas she thinks of their voiced disagreements as counterpoint:

> "Just stop, both of you," she said. "I'm tired to death of it. I'm tired of Jesse Moran and I'm tired of the two of you, repeating your same dumb arguments and niggling and bickering, Ira forever so righteous and Maggie so willing to be wrong."
> "Why . . . Fiona?" Maggie said. Her feelings were hurt. Maybe it was silly of her, but she had always secretly believed that outsiders regarded her marriage with envy. "We're not bickering; we're just discussing," she said. "We're compiling our two views of things." (311)

Tyler's subject—her specific angle on marriage—is in this novel a historical one, and *Breathing Lessons* is more concretely set in its moment in the culture than many of her other novels. For it records the sadness of the generation that came of age in the late fifties as it accepted a set of rules and lived by them, and then watched its children grow up in a world where those rules were suspended. Tyler uses the Morans' road trip the way she used Luke

174

Tull's hitchhiking expedition in *Dinner at the Homesick Restaurant*, to establish a Chaucerian breadth to her theme. She introduces, by means of near collision, a rural black family that mirrors the plight of the Morans. Mr. Otis, whom Maggie almost caused Ira to run into, has not been able to live peaceably with his wife for almost fifty years. Yet he takes pride in the longevity of their conflict; for him, the real sadness lies in the fact that his young nephew Lamont lives alone and bitter, spending his evenings in front of a television set, rather than trust another woman after his first wife.

Like Mr. Otis and his wife, Maggie and Ira have devised odd and even surly accommodations, quarreling almost as often as Ira's attention can be secured. And they disagree repeatedly in their interpretations of their own son's marital failure, his shiftlessness. People of their generation lived lives that did not meet their aspirations and then watched their own children come to a diminished adulthood in the late seventies, in the aftermath of a sexual revolution that allowed them to trade entrapment in marriage for the inability to sustain it at all.

The title *Breathing Lessons* points ironically at this brave new world. "Breathing Lessons" literally refers to the childbirth classes that Jesse and Fiona had attended when Fiona was pregnant with Leroy. Such forms of education were not available to Maggie's generation. They had to teach themselves, and only now are they gaining mastery of an action that—like love—one wants to think of as natural, involuntary.

Ironically, breathing lessons are not much help to Fiona. "Just get away with your old breathing," Fiona had told Jesse between labor pains. "I'll breathe any way I want to!" The generation of the fifties can offer no educational aides to its children, who measure the shortfall of their own aspirations and sink into bitterness, unable to summon the tenacity that earned for their parents only a compromised sort of happiness anyway.

Sinking, downward motion, is the dynamic of autumnal imagining. There are moments when Maggie acknowledges that things have gone downhill in the Moran household, to the point where her happiest days were spent with Fiona, among urine-soaked diapers and beer cans and family photographs tackily displayed in the living room. Now the family has dwindled to a rock singer who cannot keep a job and a daughter in college who does not plan to visit often. Yet the book does not end in despair, but in that calm sense of emotional stasis, a regularity of breathing that only years and the philosophic mind can bring. Among Tyler's restrainedly lyric endings, each striving somehow to offer affirmation and yet make no insupportable claims, this one may be the finest:

> Maggie spun around and returned to the bed. "Oh, Ira," she said, dropping down beside him, "what are we two going to live for, all the rest of our lives?"
> She had dislodged a stack of his cards, but he kindly refrained from straightening them and instead reached out one arm and drew her in. "There, now, sweetheart," he said, and he settled her next to him. Still holding her close, he transferred a four of spades to a five, and Maggie rested her head against his chest and watched. He had arrived at the interesting part of the game by now, she saw. He had passed that early, superficial stage when any number of moves seemed possible, and now his choices were narrower and he had to show real skill and judgment. She felt a little stir of something that came over her like a flush, a sort of inner buoyancy, and she lifted her face to kiss the warm blade of his cheekbone. Then she slipped free and moved to her side of the bed, because tomorrow they had a long car trip to make and she knew she would need a good night's sleep before they started. (326–27)

Notice that Maggie "drops down" beside Ira, at the end of a difficult day, spent in their separate yet shared measurement of losses. Yet that sense of "inner buoyancy" and the "lifting" of her face bespeak a countering force. The paragraph's quiet tension repeats the novel's metaphoric pattern, established in its title. Sinking and rising, like breathing out and breathing in, mark Maggie's earthiness, her heft. Anne Tyler's earlier protagonists operated at a greater, and a more fearful, distance from the random and dangerous worlds around them. Their emptying out of self was an effort at disembodiment. Maggie Moran marks a new, less phobic protagonist. She possesses a self that calmly empties and fills, that is limited, mortal, and therefore of—rather than opposed to—its accidental world.

BIBLIOGRAPHY

Novels by Anne Tyler

If Morning Ever Comes. New York: Alfred A. Knopf, 1964; Berkeley Books, 1983.

The Tin-Can Tree. New York: Alfred A. Knopf, 1965; Berkeley Books, 1983.

A Slipping-Down Life. New York: Alfred A. Knopf, 1970; Berkeley Books, 1983.

The Clock Winder. New York: Alfred A. Knopf, 1972; Berkeley Books, 1983.

Celestial Navigation. New York: Alfred A. Knopf, 1974; Berkeley Books, 1984.

Searching for Caleb. New York: Alfred A. Knopf, 1976; Berkeley Books, 1983.

Earthly Possessions. New York: Alfred A. Knopf, 1977; Berkeley Books, 1984.

Morgan's Passing. New York: Alfred A. Knopf, 1980; Berkeley Books, 1983.

Dinner at the Homesick Restaurant. New York: Alfred A. Knopf, 1982; Berkeley Books, 1983.

The Accidental Tourist. New York: Alfred A. Knopf, 1985.

Breathing Lessons. New York: Alfred A. Knopf, 1988.

Selected Short Stories by Anne Tyler

"Average Waves in Unprotected Waters." *New Yorker,* 28 February 1977, 32–36.

"The Bride in the Boatyard." *McCall's* 99 (June 1972): 92, 126–28.

"The Common Courtesies." *McCall's* 95 (June 1968): 62–63, 115–16.

"Dry Water." *Southern Review,* n.s. 1 (Spring 1965): 259–91.

"The Feather behind the Rock." *New Yorker,* 12 August 1967, 26–30.

"A Flaw in the Crust of the Earth." *Reporter* 37 (2 November 1967): 43–46.

"The Genuine Fur Eyelashes." *Mademoiselle* 69 (January 1967): 102–3, 136–38.

"The Geologist's Maid." *New Yorker,* 28 July 1975, 29–33.

"Half-Truths and Semi-Miracles." *Cosmopolitan* 177 (December 1974): 264–65, 269, 271, 302.

"I'm Not Going to Ask You Again." *Harper's* 231 (September 1965): 88–98.

"A Misstep of the Mind." *Seventeen* 31 (October 1972): 118–19, 170, 172.

"Outside." *Southern Review,* n.s. 7 (Autumn 1971): 1130–44.

Selected Essays and Reviews by Anne Tyler

"Because I Want More than One Life." *Washington Post,* 15 August 1976, G1, G7.

"The Fine, Full World of Welty." *Washington Star,* 26 October 1980, D1, D7.

"Olives Out of a Bottle" [Symposium at Duke University]. *Archive* 87 (Spring 1975): 70–90.

"The Poe Perplex" [Review of Julian Symons, *The Tell-Tale Heart: The Life and Works of Edgar Allan Poe]. Washington Post Book World,* 9 July 1978, E3.

"Still Just Writing." In *The Writer on Her Work: Contemporary Women Writers Reflect on Their Art and Situation,* edited by Janet Sternberg, 3–16. New York: W. W. Norton, 1980.

"A Visit with Eudora Welty." *New York Times Book Review,* 2 November 1980, 33–34.

"When the Camera Looks, It Looks for All of Us." [Review of six books of photography]. *National Observer,* 14 February 1976, 19.

"Why I Still Treasure 'The Little House.'" *New York Times Book Review,* 9 November 1986, 56.

Selected Critical Studies

Betts, Doris. "The Fiction of Anne Tyler." *Southern Quarterly* 21 (Summer 1983): 23–38.

Gardiner, Elaine, and Catherine Rainwater. "A Bibliography of Writings by Anne Tyler." In *Contemporary American Women Writers: Narrative Strategies*, edited by Catherine Rainwater and William J. Scheik, 142–52. Lexington: University of Kentucky Press, 1985.

Gullette, Margaret Morgaroth. "The Tears (and Joys) Are in the Things: Adulthood in Anne Tyler's Novels." *New England Review and Bread Loaf Quarterly* 7 (Spring 1985): 323–34. Revised as chapter 5 of *Safe at Last in the Middle Years*. Berkeley and Los Angeles: University of California Press, 1988.

Jones, Anne. "Home at Last and Homesick Again: The Ten Novels of Anne Tyler." *Hollins Critic* 23 (April 1986): 1–13.

Nesanovich, Stella. "The Individual in the Family: Anne Tyler's *Searching for Caleb* and *Earthly Possessions*. *Southern Review* 14 (Winter 1978): 170–76.

———. "The Individual in the Family: A Critical Introduction to the Novels of Anne Tyler." Ph.D. diss., Louisiana State University, 1979.

———. "An Anne Tyler Checklist, 1959–80." *Bulletin of Bibliography* 38 (April–June 1981): 53–64.

Ridley, Clifford. "Anne Tyler: A Sense of Reticence Balanced by 'Oh, Well, Why Not?' " *National Observer* 11 (22 July 1972): 23.

Robertson, Mary F. "Anne Tyler: Medusa Points and Contact Points." In *Contemporary American Women Writers: Narrative Strategies*, edited by Catherine Rainwater and William J. Scheik, 119–42. Lexington: University of Kentucky Press, 1985.

Updike, John. "Family Ways" [Review of *Searching for Caleb*]. *New Yorker*, 29 March 1976, 110–112.

————. "Loosened Roots" [Review of *Earthly Possessions*]. *New Yorker,* 6 June 1977, 130–34.

————. "Imagining Things" [Review of *Morgan's Passing*]. *New Yorker,* 23 June 1980, 97–101.

————. "On Such a Beautiful Green Little Planet" [Review of *Dinner at the Homesick Restaurant*]. *New Yorker,* 5 April 1982, 193–97.

————. "Leaving Home" [Review of *The Accidental Tourist*]. *New Yorker,* 28 October 1985, 85, 106–11.

(Four of these reviews, "Family Ways," "Loosened Roots," "Imagining Things," and "On such a Beautiful Green Little Planet," are reprinted in *Hugging the Shore,* 273–99. New York: Random House, 1983.)

INDEX

Accident: in Flannery
O'Connor's and Tyler's
fiction, 10–11; observed
by Tyler in Welty's fic-
tion, 28; Macon Leary's
response to, 149, 162–63;
Maggie Moran recon-
ciled to, 179

Accidental Tourist, The:
Freudian concept of
death instincts in, 11, 13,
148–58; accident in, 149,
161–63; role of nonverbal
communication in,
159–62

Agoraphobia: as philo-
sophic and paradoxical
complex of ideas, 50–53;
Freud on, 51; as condi-
tion of Tyler's artist-
protagonists, 17, 36; as
imaginative premise for
Tyler's fictions, 71–72,
147–49; defined as
panic-avoidance, 73;
agora as market, 85, 92

Allen, Woody: his concept
of "Anhedonia" and
Cody Tull, 140

Baltzell, E. Digby: on Quaker vs. Puritan culture,
1–2; on Quaker indif-
ference to sexuality, 2;
on aristocracy, 93, 103;
on WASP reclusion, 94

Breathing Lessons: as Keatsian response to mortal-
ity, 14; Maggie Moran
as Keats's "Autumn,"
166; home movies as
Grecian urn, 167

"Bride in the Boatyard, The"
(short story), 33

Brown, Gillian: on role of
gender in agoraphobia,
92n

Celestial Navigation: marks
maturation of Tyler's
technique, 6; as a
"Poetics" of agorapho-
bia, 12–13, 87; origins of
Tyler's reticent male
protagonists, 69–70; as
metafiction, 71, 87; art
as inventory in, 73,
79–80; agoraphobia as
paradox in, 81; solip-
sism of Mary Tell, 84;
agora as market in, 85;
compared to *Morgan's
Passing,* 87

Clockwinder, The: initiates
stylistic middle period,
12; character as palimp-
sest in, 48; agoraphobia
as idea in, 50–53; ob-
verseness of victim and
savior in, 53–56; com-
pared to short story "A
Misstep of the Mind,"
53–55; compared to short
story "Half Truths and
Semi-Miracles," 55–56;
density of texture in, 61;
contrasted to Flannery
O'Connor's "Every-
thing That Rises Must
Converge," 64; Tyler on
Elizabeth's fate, 65

Cornell, Joseph: as analog to Jeremy Pauling, 75n

Dinner at the Homesick Restaurant: idealization in, 13, 125–31; Zeno of Elea as influence on idea of time, 131–37; time as occasion vs. time as duration in, 137–46
"Dry Water" (short story), 43n, 147

Earthly Possessions: Quaker sensibility in, 7–8, 124; idealization in, 13, 115–17; chiasmus as narrative structure, 116; scriptural origins of title, 118–19; Christianity in, 120–24

Faulkner, William: and Southern writing, 12; echoed in *If Morning Ever Comes,* 20–21; echoed in *Celestial Navigation,* 79; echoed in *Earthly Possessions,* 113
"Flaw in the Crust of the Earth, A" (short story), 147
Freud, Sigmund: theory of death instincts, 13, 148–58; on agoraphobia, 51

García Márquez, Gabriel: Tyler's admiration for, 71; influence on *Searching for Caleb,* 89–91
"Genuine Fur Eyelashes, The" (short story), 43n

"Half-Truths and Semi-Miracles" (short story), 55–56

If Morning Ever Comes: domesticity as subject, 12; dreams in, 17–20; cinematic time in, 19; Faulkner in, 20–21; palimpsest as structure of, 24ff
Idealization, 13; defined, 115–16; as diagnosis of Tull children, 126–31
"I'm Not Going to Ask You Again" (short story), 108

Jones, Anne: on Southern sexual code, 24n; on Narcissism, 125

Kohut, Heinz: on idealization and narcissism, 115–16

"Misstep of the Mind, A" (short story), 53–55
Morgan's Passing: abstractness of, 12, 87–88; Morgan as inverse agoraphobe, 53

Narcissism: as explanation of Tyler's characters, 125n; in idealization, 115–16

O'Connor, Flannery: authorial cruelty of, 10; "accident" in, 10; echoed in *Clockwinder,* 64; in Tyler's short stories, 110; Tyler subverts Christian absolutism of, 111
"Outside" (short story), 147

Poe, Edgar Allen: echoed in *If Morning Ever Comes,* 21; Tyler describes his psyche as palimpsest, 49

Price, Reynolds: as Tyler's teacher, 8

Searching for Caleb: patterns of history and genetics, 13, 92–95; compared to García Márquez's *One Hundred Years of Solitude,* 89–91; working-class characters in, 101–3; technique of as kaleidoscope, 104–5

Slipping-Down Life, A: as naturalism, 12, 41; published in *Redbook,* 40; account of Evie's scar compared to *Redbook* version, 45–47

Time: in *If Morning Ever Comes,* 19; in *The Clock Winder,* 48–48; in *Dinner at the Homesick Restaurant,* 131–46; in *Accidental Tourist,* 163–64; in *Breathing Lessons,* 167

Tin Can Tree, The: as minimalist, 122; characters as artists, 29ff; photography as metaphor, 27, 32–35; pointillistic dialogue in, 37–39

Tyler, Anne: early life in Quaker commune, 2–3; nature of autobiographical testimony, 67; parts of herself in Jeremy Pauling, 69, 72; account of her working day, 82

Updike, John: Puritan style compared to Tyler's Quaker style, 2–8; notes Tyler's lack of obsession, 5–6; rendering of consciousness in *Rabbit Is Rich,* 4–5; notes Tyler's authorial benevolence, 107; compares Tyler to Flannery O'Connor, 112

Welty, Eudora: as influence, 8–9, 15; Southernness of, 9; fiction as halted film, 28; echoed in short story, 108; her "A Memory" as agoraphobic fiction, 109

Zeno of Elea: and Tyler's concept of time in *Dinner at the Homesick Restaurant,* 133–37